The Voice of Spirit

Other titles by the author:

The Voice of Spirit: A Medium's Story

The Voice of Spirit

The World Through My Eyes

Judy O'Brien

Copyright © Judy O'Brien 2020

All rights reserved. This book may not be reproduced in whole or part, stored, posted on the internet, or transmitted in any form or by any means, electronic, mechanical, photocopying, recording, or other, except brief extracts for the purpose of review, without written permission from the author of this book.

Disclaimer

This book is sold with the understanding that the author is not offering specific personal advice to the reader. The author disclaims any responsibility for liability, loss or risk, personal or otherwise, that happens as a consequence of the use and application of any of the content of this book. The author has made every effort to ensure the accuracy of the information within this book was correct at time of publication.

Some names have been changed to protect the identity of individuals who have shared their story.

Front cover illustration © Wendy Grace Mackay
Typeset by BookPOD

ISBN: 978-0-6487533-0-8 (pbk) 978-0-6487533-1-5 (e-book)

A catalogue record for this book is available from the National Library of Australia

Dedication

*I have never understood the phrase,
labour of love, until now...*

This book is dedicated to all those whom I love and who have walked with me on my life's journey. How I saw the world through my eyes was totally different before I started as a professional medium and as a physical being. I do not see the world as one dimensional, but as a series of experiences and memories that have been created to help develop my spiritual growth. Through these various learnings, both physical and spiritual, I have transformed into a more confident, compassionate and soulful person. Working with spirit isn't a career, it is a way of life, and one I do not take for granted.

I am extremely honoured to be a voice for our loved ones in Heaven and other spiritual beings, such as Angels and Spirit Guides. It is through their work that my life has become richer and more fulfilled. With knowledge comes understanding and it has led me on a path of self-discovery, helping me to find my life's purpose.

To every client, audience member, and the people who have read my first book, you, the reader and the people who have touched my life and assisted me to fulfil my life's purpose: it is with deep gratitude I say thank you, what you have contributed to my life is unimaginable. You have contributed more to my life and to my soul's journey, than I can ever repay. I now see life differently with an open heart and an open mind.

To the spiritual beings I have been introduced to, and those I'm yet to meet, I look forward to working with you and connecting with your energy in the future.

To God, thank you for teaching me to respect your time, myself and all the lessons I had to work through in order to finish this book. I thank you for this beautiful gift you have bestowed upon me. May your light and love shine through me always.

Acknowledgments

Throughout this book, I refer to the angels as "my angels" - but I certainly claim no ownership over them. They are God's angels and spiritual messengers. They are available to everyone who calls upon them or who can communicate with them. During the times in my life when I have called on them for guidance, unconditional support and protection, they have never failed me, and this is illustrated in this book. So please excuse my reference to "my angels". I say it, not as a form of possession, but out of endearment and love.

I speak of God frequently throughout this book because I believe my gift comes from God. Everyone has their own journey to fulfil, their beliefs are theirs alone, and will no doubt differ to mine. I believe it doesn't matter who you pray to or have faith in as long as we respect each other's point of view or belief system without prejudice or judgement. We all have individualistic gifts and our journey is our own to take and grow from.

I love this part of the book because I get to express my sincerest appreciation to the people and spiritual beings who have impacted my life. Words cannot be expressed how grateful I am to have them in my life. Their unwavering faith in my ability is incredible and their reassurance to keep moving forward when things seemed overwhelming is encouraging.

To my husband, Darrin, your unconditional love and support is inspiring. You continue to believe in me even when I don't. Our love grows every day.

To my children, Cameron, Elyse and Brooklyn, you are my life source and I thank you for your unconditional love and support. You have taught me many things, and I have spoken about some of them in this book. This is dedicated to the three of you, and I thank you for allowing me to share your stories. It is a privilege to be your mum.

To my mum, dad and my extended family members, thank you for your encouragement and unconditional love and support. I stand on my own two feet with pride knowing that you are supporting me in all my endeavours.

To Rose, my mentor and friend. There are no words that I can say to express my gratitude. You have been there to help facilitate my spiritual growth, with unconditional love and you always give me a gentle nudge when things seem overwhelming.

To my Guardian Angels, you know who you are. You have believed in me and have helped to shape the person I am today. Thank you for your continuing friendship and you have helped me to have faith in myself, on a daily basis.

Lastly, thank you to the beautiful people and their spiritual families who have blessed my life by allowing me to share their precious stories. One of the best parts of my gift that it has enabled me to meet such incredible people who have opened their lives to me, and allowed the spirit to share their stories with their loved ones.

And finally, to you, the reader. Thank you for taking the time to read my story. May it give you insights into the life of a medium, and through my stories you see the world through my eyes. May the chapters within these pages give you peace and comfort knowing there is life after life and that we never die. Without spirit, these stories would not be told, and they illustrate that life is eternal. I hope you can resonate with some or all my stories and take what you need from them and enjoy reading this book as much as I have enjoyed writing it.

Contents

Foreword ... xi

Part One

1. A Soul's Journey Home ... 3
2. Everything Happens at The Right Time ... 9
3. Being Real ... 11
4. Grateful for the Experience ... 13
5. Wanting the World and Knowing Where You're At ... 23
6. Who Am I? ... 27
7. Taking Responsibility ... 35
8. Accountability ... 41
9. Respectful Behaviour ... 47
10. Something Worth Pondering ... 49
11. Judgement ... 51
12. What's the Old Saying? Patience is a Virtue ... 57
13. Spirit Always Knows Best ... 63
14. Spirit is in Control ... 69
15. Gain, Learn, Know & Understand ... 73
16. Knowing the Right Time to Communicate with Spirit ... 81
17. Inspirational Story ... 89
18. Blueprints ... 97
19. How Do Our Loved Ones Know Our Vibration and When to Come to Us? ... 99

20	Having Faith in Yourself and in Spirit	103
21	Seeing Through the Eyes of Our Loved Ones	107
22	Random Messages	113
23	Guilt versus Regret	121
24	Grief	123
25	The Power of Prayer	131
26	We Are Never Alone	139
27	Knowing the Right Time to Communicate with Spirit	143

Part Two

28	Memorable Short Stories about Connections With Our Loved Ones Who Have Crossed Over	149
29	The Gift of Life	151
30	Labour of Love	169

Foreword

Judy O'Brien is a well-respected highly sought after Australian medium who has continued to build her reputation for over fifteen years.

I first met Judy as a sceptical client back in 2006 when she connected me with my grandfather who had recently passed. One of the first things Judy ever said to me was there was a woman standing behind me holding her hands up and moving them around saying:

"Look what I can do now." This was the moment a sceptic became a believer, as I knew this was my Aunty Phil (my grandmother's sister) who had passed away before I was born after suffering an extreme form of arthritis where she was unable to lift or move her hands.

Over the now many years we have known each other, Judy has become my best friend, confidant, godmother to my son and soul sister. Judy's humble, friendly and empathetic nature is what draws people to her and her ability to use her unique gift to provide messages of love and light to her clients is why her clientele continues to grow. Unlike her first book, *Voice of Spirit* which detailed some of her favourite client readings, Judy's latest book is highly personal and speaks of her spiritual growth and learnings throughout her career.

The Voice of Spirit: The World Through My Eyes provides the reader personal insights into the world through Judy's eyes and how she has learned to accept, love and embrace her gift throughout her spiritual journey. The purpose of sharing these personal experiences is not only to provide the reader an understanding of what Judy's life has been like, but also an opportunity for Judy to understand and accept herself.

I look forward to Judy's continued success both professionally and personally.

Belief, acceptance and love.
Emma Carter

Part One

1

A Soul's Journey Home

If someone would have told me five years ago that I would be sitting down and writing my second book, I would have thought they were mad. Well, here I am! In May 2016 my first book, *The Voice of Spirit*, was published, I was so excited because it was finally here after waiting five years to be completed, but I was also apprehensive at the same time. For five years, it was a work in progress, and when the book was in my hands, I thought... here it is. I love it, but oh my goodness, I hope people love it as much as I do. I was very aware that I was putting myself out there, and I was feeling totally exposed because I wrote about myself and the memories and moments that were personal to me. The book received great reviews and everyone I talked to would express their love for it. They couldn't put it down, once they started to read it. Which was great, because the stories I wrote about were ones that I held close to my heart. It was even talked about overseas. When I was notified about this, I thought, wow! Not bad for an Aussie mum from the suburbs of Western Sydney.

Leading up to the publication of my book, I received a lot of messages from people asking me questions about spirit, "How do I know that the signs I'm getting are from spirit and not my imagination?" or "How do I let go and move forward?"

So, I sat down one day and realised that the purpose for writing my book was to provide a guideline for when people feel stuck or confused as to where their life is travelling or a reference to understanding spirit, and how we work together. I thought about it and the penny dropped. I had been asked so many questions from many people throughout my career as a medium and I didn't realise as I was writing my book, I could give the answers to people in the form of a book. I know the answers I give are what I believed and may not resonate with some people, but to be used as a reference would be great. It's like anything, I believe what you get out of something is what you need at the time.

One day I was talking to my friend Bek, she was telling me how on the day of her sister's graduation from high school, she was reading my book, and in particular, the chapter on signs from heaven. Bek was very close with her grandfather, they spent a lot of time together whilst she was growing up. In her adult years, they were inseparable. The year before her sister's graduation, her grandfather had passed away and this devastated Bek. On the day of her sisters graduation from High School, Bek along with her family, arrived home from the ceremony and to relax, Bek picked up my book, and started to read the chapter called "Signs From Heaven". The next minute, she heard a song being played in the other room and she noticed her sister's iPhone had just turned itself on to play the music. The fact that no-one had touched the iPhone or was near it was amazing. The song that was playing was *You Are Not Alone* by Michael Jackson.

Bek's grandmother attended the graduation as well and after the ceremony, she was talking about how she missed her husband. I was so excited for Bek and after she finished telling me the story, I thought wow, that's amazing, how Bek's grandfather had let his family know they were never alone only strengthened my belief in spirit, and no matter when it happens, spirit will always let you know they are okay. It may not be in the way you want them to let you know, but it will be in the way they want too. In my experience, it is when you least expect it, nine times out of ten you need that comfort at that precise moment.

Another sign I received my book was on the right track and should be used as guidance came when I first received the shipment of books. I opened the box, and I was giddy with excitement! I put the book in my reading room to show a client and their mum because they knew I was writing one. My client came sat down with her mum and I started to give information from their loved ones, and in particular her grandfather they were close too. Halfway into the reading, the grandfather told me to pick up my book and go to the chapter "Letting Go" and show this to his granddaughter. At first, I thought it was my ego talking because I had it in my mind to show them the book after the session. I didn't want my clients to think I was up myself and showing off my new book. As time went on during the reading, the grandfather became more insistent and asked me again if I could open my book to the chapter he spoke about. I paused during the reading contemplating my next move and I thought *I'm just going to say it,* because I knew better than to question spirit. They always know best.

I relayed the message from the grandfather to the granddaughter and opened my book to the chapter "Letting Go". I realised I had been discussing this with my client already, and when I showed them the page, the mother asked

"What page number was that?"

"Fifty-five." The mother looked stunned, and she began to tell me that her father was a fire fighter and the number for his helmet was fifty-five, the fire station was fifty-five and his funeral plot was numbered fifty-five. I stared at the mother, and instantly knew at that moment that we all experienced something special and I was so grateful to spirit for letting me know, they would help me give the right information to my clients and to listen to them sooner!

Soul's Journey

One day over a cup of coffee with my friend and mentor, Rose, we were discussing content for my second book, and out of the blue, Rose said the title of my second book would be *A Soul's Journey Home*

"Yes!" I said. I loved it because it resonated with me at the soul level and I instantly knew that was the title. I had previously had a different title: *You Are What You Think*, But I decided to have it as a chapter title instead. I love going for a coffee with Rose, because not only do we have a laugh, but she is the one person who gets me and my quirky ways. I'm not saying that my family do not understand me or love me, especially my husband Darrin, who knows me like the back of his hand. He is one of my biggest supporters and I credit my achievements to him. My kids usually roll their eyes.

"There goes mum again," they'd say, as all children do when their mum is being herself and her quirkiness comes out.

As you can see, the title of this book is *The Voice of Spirit: The World Through My Eyes*. I decided to change the title because I realised the content of this book focusses on how I see the world and the experiences I have had, have shaped the person I am today.

Another thing Rose gets is what I call "Judy Talk." This isn't a special language I have adopted or introduced to people. It's just that some things need to be explained in a certain way for me to understand the meaning or reference, and because Rose and I are connected energetically, it's easier for me to understand her. My poor husband gets frustrated with me because he will explain a situation or subject, and my eyes will glaze over, and nine times out of ten, he has lost my attention in the first sentence. This is not to say he can't explain things to me, or that he isn't a good communicator, because he is. Darrin is finishing his course in Life Coaching. He is very good with explaining it to others and maybe because I am his wife and too close to him, I don't always understand him. I also considered that I don't want to see myself as his client. I am not a person who is qualified in this area of expertise. I just *know* when Rose explains something it makes sense. Darrin usually gets frustrated after explaining something for ten minutes:

"Go visit Rose or give her a call".

At the time, we were discussing our soul's purpose, and why we were here in the physical world. As I have previously mentioned, our soul's purpose is to learn through experiences and being in the moment. A moment I believe is being where you are and doing exactly what you are meant to be doing in order for the future events to unfold or progress the way they are meant to. When you say to yourself:

"I'm where I need to be, doing exactly what I am meant to be doing," you are allowing energy to flow freely because you are not subconsciously blocking any opportunity that comes your way. I must stress that I am not a trained psychologist or psychiatrist, and this might differ for each individual. I have used this mantra or phrase every day and especially when I get confused with life and my direction in life. I can be impatient sometimes and I'm sure I'm not the only one; maybe you, the reader, can agree with this as you might have found yourself in a situation where patience was necessary.

Whenever I discuss what a moment is with a client, I remember what spirit had taught me. I don't know who specifically said this, but I was sure the council of guides had a hand in it. They said:

"We are all born spiritual, because we are born with a soul and a spirit. But it is up to us to decide whether or not we are going to use our intuition (gut feeling) or not." There is no right answer or wrong answer as it is up to the individual to choose. If a person uses their intuition in their daily lives, which means listening to what it is saying or feeling (If it doesn't feel right, it isn't), they are considered spiritual because they are using their spirit or inner voice. A person who doesn't want to use their inner voice or intuition and puts blocks up is considered a sceptic. If you place blocks or walls in front of you in life, then you are not able to or willing to have an open mind as to what lies in front of you. If you think only negative thoughts, you will most likely be in a negative situation or receive negativity.

2

Everything Happens at The Right Time

During the process of editing my first book, it took a while to complete as my editor not only had to finish this, but she had to work full time and look after her family. We would often correspond by phone call and emails, and she noted a few times that she was sorry it was taking so long to get finished.

"*It will be finished in its own time and when the time is right,*" I would say to her, so I wouldn't stress. Which is mainly thanks to my friend and mentor, Rose. Quite often in the past I would get a little impatient.

"When will my book be done?"

"It will be finished when it's the right time," she would reply. Now for a person that is sometimes impatient and controlling, this was like waving a red flag in front of a bull. Over the years, I have improved because I have learnt from Rose and spirit that everything happens in God's Time and this does not necessarily match my time. How often have you, the reader, wanted something so badly, for example a piece of clothing and just gone and bought it without weighing up the pros and cons and realised later that you should've shopped around because you may have seen something better and cheaper in another store?

Everything happens in the right time was validated when the editing of my book was complete, and it involved my dad. I was asked many years ago why I was writing a book, and my answer was always the same. I wanted to tell spirit's story and show how amazing spirit is, but in truth, the main reason I wrote was for my dad. I have always remembered my dad being an avid reader, and I imagined him reading my book one day. Just before I started writing, my dad was diagnosed with cancer and after he recovered, I knew I must get it finished, because I didn't know what lay ahead. In September 2015, I was corresponding with my editor and she apologised for the length of time the editing was taking, and I realised that it would happen in the right time. In December of that year, my dad needed emergency eye surgery to remove a cataract from his right eye and because the left eye needed surgery as well, he was scheduled to have his left eye operated on in March 2016. Exactly a week later after dad's second eye operation, I opened my emails and my manuscript was complete. My husband Darrin raced to a printing store, printed the manuscript and arranged it in a folder. I drove to my mum and dad's place and handed dad my book. Now I understood why spirit was taking longer than I had planned. I realised my dad could read it with improved vision now, whereas before he may have struggled. I knew there was a reason for the delay, and it was perfect timing.

3

Being Real

Every day we as human beings are presented with opportunities to help us grow and learn. I believe life isn't about money, fame, or fortune. It's about being real and accepting the situation or the person we are or that we are going to become. My favourite quote is from an unknown author from Quotling.com:

"A meaningful life is not being rich, being popular or being perfect. It's about being real, being humble, being able to share ourselves, and touch the lives of others." That's what I strive to do every day. There is a part in every one of us that would like to have fame and fortune, or to be well-known, and in May 2017, I had to re-evaluate what I wanted in life. I began by looking back over the past seven years of my mediumship, let me tell you, I didn't know I had accomplished so much in that time, even though I thought I hadn't. The things I had done and accomplished were amazing, and I thanked spirit for the opportunities. Over the past few years, my reputation had grown, and I was becoming well known, not only in Sydney but other states as well.

"You know you could be big mum," my son said to me one day. I looked at him and thought *What does it mean to be big? Does it mean making a lot of money? Travelling to different places? Being recognised throughout Australia or the world? and what does it mean to be celebrated?* As I have said, who wouldn't like to be recognised and well-known for their profession? Most of the time, we strive to be the best in our field, whether it is a career or sporting activity. I'm sure I'm not the only person to imagine being famous when I was a little girl. I dreamed of performing in the Australian Ballet. Of course, that didn't happen.

What I have noticed in my profession is that a lot of people will have opinions about who is the best reader, and I have seen a person write on a medium's advertising page that this particular person was the best, because they had seen them all. I thought to myself it was strange, because I was pretty sure they hadn't seen everyone in the whole world.

4

Grateful for the Experience

When people meet me for the first time, I come across as a person who is confident, intellectual and assertive in my work. Little do they know that my insecurities and vulnerability are bubbling just under the surface. I have mentioned before that I always become nervous before every reading, both privately and publicly. I am sure God and my Angels are smiling as I say the same prayer before I start each reading:

"Please God and my Angels, please, please let someone come through for my clients." Thankfully, the loved ones in spirit are awesome, and come through with flying colours each time, and I am very blessed to have them with us.

I am very honoured to have been born with my gift, and I am very blessed to receive emails, texts and messages thanking me for being their loved one's voice during my readings. My response is always the same.

"I thank God every day for this gift, and I thank him equally for the people I meet." Without spirit I would not be me and to be their voice is a godsend.

In May 2018, I knew I was transforming, both physically and spiritually. In November of that year, I met a wonderful reader called Yoe, and I had an impromptu reading from her. Whenever I go for a reading, I feel the pull to do so, I go without hesitation, because I know this is my Angel's way of showing me the direction I need to take or letting me know I am on the right path. Yoe used cards in her reading for me, and I could relate to everything that spirit said. She said I would be going through a transformation, but she didn't elaborate on how, or when it would happen, or even what it would be. Four months after the reading, I realised spirit was spot on. I *was* going through a transformation, but not just spiritually. It was a physical transformation that had begun, and in turn, it helped to balance my spiritual side, and ultimately enhanced my spiritual growth. I started wearing my hair differently, exercising more, meditating regularly and my diet had changed for the better.

Spirit has taught me that we have two bodies, and both are equally important. We have the physical body that we were born into, and it is important to take care of it for the years we are meant to be in the physical world. It is up to us to take care of it and give it nourishment. Our body is like a car: if you don't service it regularly, then it will eventually break down. Servicing means giving it nourishment and getting the right help it needs if it is unwell. Our spiritual body is what we have been born with - our soul. It equally needs nourishment, and this means recharging the batteries when needed. This could include: having a spiritual cleansing, having fun and enjoying life, meditating, looking at life, smelling life and living life. Our emotions and how we feel are important for our spiritual body as well. In other words, nourishing and looking after the spiritual body means cleansing the soul. As physical beings we need to balance both bodies and even though we give attention to one body, we must be considerate of the other body and feed it as well. Transformation doesn't necessarily mean spiritual growth because the physical growth is important as well. At the time, my physical growth was important, and I realised I had not been looking after my body and I was becoming lethargic and unhappy. In my family's history, heart attacks and strokes are very common, along with diabetes and high cholesterol. I was unhappy with my appearance, and I knew I couldn't afford to have plastic surgery, so it was up to me to change my mindset and start doing something about it. So, I changed my dietary behaviours. I have always worn my hair with a fringe, and during one week of readings, my fringe was irritating me: it was constantly getting in my eyes, even though I had cut it. Then one day it was frustrating me again and I heard spirit say:

"It's blocking your third eye." I decided to wear my hair differently - without a fringe, and of course spirit was right, my sight became clearer and I could understand completely what spirit was showing me. The funny thing was, I had more people complimenting me on the way I wore my hair. Exercising, well it goes without saying: it's better for the body, and I started Pilates. I started a course online, and meditation was the key element, and this would help with my spiritual growth. So, my transformation had commenced and one thing I have learnt from spirit is, you may think you know what path spirit wants you to be on, but in my experience, spirit likes to surprise you and take another path and they always know best.

For me, May 2018 was a reflective month, and the daily running around after our children was normal, and I was quite busy with my work. One day I was driving home from shopping and I realised, I wasn't practicing what I preached, I wasn't looking at life, smelling life and living life. Because life is so busy and hectic for many people these days, we rarely do the things that bring peace, joy or contentment in our lives, because we are too focused on the future, without living in the moment and enjoying life and what it has to offer. Creating memories and being in the moment is so important along with being grateful for the things we have and experience. I was so preoccupied with life, I sometimes felt I that had no time for myself and this made me feel a little resentful at times and of course, the ego rears its ugly head, and I feel unappreciated and tired.

For the past three years, I have been performing mediumship events in clubs and cafes as well as private readings. I like doing this because it is rewarding, it gives me great satisfaction to relay messages from our loved ones to a larger group of people, even though not everyone is guaranteed a reading. I have always been a very private person, and I prefer to keep to myself a lot of the time. I don't like to look at Facebook or other social networks to see what other people in my industry are up too. However, one day I was taking a brief look at Facebook, and I noticed an abundance of mediums advertising events at various clubs around Sydney. At the time, I was thinking of an event coming up later in the year that we were organising south of Sydney. *Why would people want to come and see me in an event when there are a lot of other people doing these events already? Why was I different?* I thought to myself. I wasn't jealous or envious towards these people, because I was happy that different people were revealing their gifts and to see like-minded people out there was awesome. I thought about the significance of mediums going to clubs or cafés, which led me to feeling insecure and second guessing myself, I said to myself:

"If all these people are doing these shows, why should I be doing them?" Everywhere I looked, social media was advertising something regarding mediumship events. Then out of know where, I had a voice in my head telling me to be appreciative of the things I have now and in this moment. I recognised I was being selfish, and that I wanted to know what I wanted and, I had questioned what spirit had in store for me. In other words, patience wasn't my friend at that time. I became conscious of the fact I wasn't appreciating what God had given me already regarding my personal readings, as I was fully booked. I had been so focused on what other people were up too, that I forgot what truly matters - me.

Because I was looking into the future, I was neglecting what mattered to me the most. I hadn't appreciated what God had given me in the first place: a gift that brings peace to people. So, I said a prayer of appreciation to God and my Angels, thanking them for the spirits I had met and were yet to meet and the people who wanted to come and see me for private readings.

The instant I said my prayer of gratitude, a small truck driving on the opposite side of the road, started to bunny hop right next to me and the driver was looking straight at me, smiling and nodding his head. My first reaction was to call him an idiot, because I thought what he was doing on the road was dangerous; however, I noticed no other cars were on the road. This was a big sign from God and my Angels, and they were saying thank you for the prayer and appreciation.

Sometimes when we are trying to get ahead in life, we concentrate on wanting to know what the future holds for us and trying to control a situation that is sometimes out of our control. In doing so, we get bogged down with our thoughts and expectations, and we become frustrated when things don't go according to our plan. We need to *see* life and appreciate where we are. Life is a collection of moments, and we need to experience each one to help us grow and evolve as a spiritual being. Remaining in the moment allows us to appreciate what we have, and when you are in the moment, opportunities don't pass you by, they help us grow physically and spiritually.

Food for the Soul

I was talking to my mentor and friend, Rose, one day regarding mediumship and why we do what we do.

"Communicating with spirit, however you do it because there is no right or wrong way, it should feed the soul," she said to me.

I thought this was very profound, and I realised that I am doing what I am meant to do, working with my Angels, spirits and other spiritual beings, is food for my soul that gives me daily nourishment, and it should be used with integrity and in the right context. My Aunty Janet, my godmother and a minister's wife gave me a Bible, and in it she wrote

"Judy, always remember, the Bible is meant to be bread for daily use and not cake for special occasions." Just as food is described as any nutritious substance that people or animals eat or drink to maintain life and growth, working with spirit helps sustain my physical body, and contributes to the growth of my soul. In life we are encouraged to keep our physical body in tip-top shape, eat good food, get plenty of exercise and relaxation. It is very true with our spiritual body, and crucial to doing the work of a medium. I must constantly feed my soul with positive affirmations, connecting to spirit through the right channel, maintaining integrity and doing the right thing by spirit. I am forever learning and evolving as a spiritual being. I must also have time out to relax and recharge my batteries so I can continue with the work I love to do.

Individuals who do not do this work daily or professionally like myself may not understand what it is like to be me, and what I must achieve to be a voice for spirit. I always say that an hour-long reading is equivalent to four hours work, as it is both mentally and physically challenging. But working with spirit is a passion, and something I am very grateful for. I have had clients say how tiring it must be to be a medium after a session, and yes they are correct: most days at the end of my working day, I am in bed having a quick sleep before I have to take my children somewhere or cook dinner or doing the mum thing and most of the time, my sleep is at three p.m.

Understanding yourself and trusting in the work that you do is vitally important when you are a medium. I cannot talk for all mediums, but I can talk about my own experiences. Some of you may resonate what I am saying, and some of you may not, and that is okay. Because everyone learns and grows differently.

Over the years, I have had many people ask me how I communicate with spirit and my response is always the same: I trust in what I am being told. Whether I am seeing a picture in front of me, or in my mind, receiving a thought, or hearing someone talking to me. Being drawn to different signs, such as, a statue of a piano in my reading room, and when I am drawn to look at it, I ask my client if they played or someone played piano in the past. If they say yes, I know that was a sign from spirit. If I hear songs in my head or on the radio, I know they are significant for someone or myself. I will know the answer when the right time approaches. When spirit wants you to know something, they will bother you until you understand what they are trying to tell you. This happened to my friend Bek. One day her grandfather came to me from spirit and he asked me to get in contact with Bek and give her a message from him. So, I messaged her, and I asked if she could comprehend it.

"No," she said. I asked her to let it go and she will hopefully understand the message when the time was right. A few days later Bek came and saw me and said she was sitting at home, deleting messages on her mobile phone and she was trying to delete my message, but every time she went to delete it, the message wouldn't delete, and she was compelled to look at her grandfather's message again. Bek worked through the possibilities of what it could be, and every time she was incorrect the message wouldn't delete, until finally she understood her grandfather's message. As soon as she "got it" - the message deleted instantly. Spirit always knows best. We just need to trust when the time is right, we will be shown the answer.

In my experience, when we are given a message from spirit and at the time, we do not have any idea what they are talking about, they will always be correct. We need to have faith, and all will be revealed in the right time. I have on numerous occasions, when Rose gave me a message, I replied with:

"Don't be so daft, Rose," and when the time was right, I understood the message that I needed to go back to her (with my tail between my legs), and say spirit was right. During one reading I had with Rose, she told me my dad would say to me how proud he was of me and what I was doing, and at the time I thought Rose and spirit had lost the plot or their minds, because my dad had never been interested in the spirit world or the work I do:

this is why I hid what I could do for many years. I am not saying my dad is a horrible or judgemental person because he is not; he is a loving and beautiful dad. I just couldn't see him accepting the work I do. Then, one day I was on the phone with my dad, and he was talking about his friend who had been diagnosed with liver cancer and was on the mend. Spirit compelled me to tell him his friend still had cancer and it had spread to his stomach, but that it wasn't diagnosed yet and it wouldn't be a great outcome.

"I think you are wrong," my dad said, and I left it at that. A few weeks later my dad called me and said his friend had just come back from his specialist appointment and the cancer was detected in his stomach and it was not a great prognosis. The next thing dad said stopped me in my tracks. He said how proud he was of me and the work I am doing. Of course, I called Rose the next day and said spirit was right.

Trusting, I believe, in yourself and spirit is the fundamental element to working with spirit. It is not the only element; it is the foundation. To trust in spirit, you need to have trust in yourself first, because spirit is in each one of us. *"We are all born with a spirit and a soul."*

People who are considered spiritual choose to use what they have been given from God -their intuition, and the people who are considered sceptical choose not to use their intuition. In most cases, they block any information they receive from spirit. They say no to these messages. In my belief, this is not a bad thing, because we need to have balance in life. In my experience, it is much easier to listen to our intuition, even if we do not like what it is telling us and not ignore it. Having sceptical people in the world allows us to help them see the world or situations in a different way. It may not be a better way, but it will give us time to reflect and see what we can improve both on a global or individual scale. In turn, the sceptical person can teach the spiritual person what happens when we block information sent to us by spirit, and the consequences we face when we do not listen to our intuition. Life isn't always black and white, there are grey areas, but it is what we accomplish in life - whether it is small or large that is the important thing. It is not the end or beginning of the journey that is important, it is what you do on that journey that is vital to your growth as an evolved soul. We as individuals will always go through things in our lives, and the timing of these events is sometimes irrelevant to the spirit world. It is up to the person how long they want to stay stuck in the mud for or move forward to our destination. When something doesn't go according to your plan in life, do you sit down and chuck a tantrum? Or do you stand up, brush yourself off and keep moving forward even though you don't know when this part of your life's journey will end or change again?

We as individuals have the power to work through our lessons in life. There are some lessons that are out of our control because they are already written in our contract before we arrive on earth, but it is our choice whether we want to change our behaviour and thought processes for other lessons and challenges. Life isn't meant to be easy, there will always be pitfalls and challenges, but it is what we do with these experiences that matter.

Experiences create memories, and memories will last in this lifetime, and in the next. The most important thing is that we learn our lessons, and if we can help other people who might be experiencing the same challenges, that is a bonus. A song by Beyoncé has been influential for me over the past few months. It is called *I Was Here*. It is a very powerful song, and everyone interprets the lyrics in ways that are important to them. To me, the song represents a person's life, and one day after hearing it, I sat down and thought about my life and the people I have met, and the impact I have had on their lives, and their impact on mine. I have been fortunate enough to meet beautiful people, and spirits, and I have learnt a great deal about myself, and working with spirit. After listening to the song, I felt that it resonated with a person's completion of their life. I thought about how I wanted to be remembered, and about the people I had touched with spiritual messages from their loved ones. It didn't matter if I was famous or well-off, all that mattered was that I was here, like the song, and that I made my mark. If one person remembered I was here on this earth that would be enough because being here isn't about money, fame or fortune. It is being on earth to grow and learn as an evolved soul, and if you are lucky enough to touch people's lives, even if it is many or one at a time, you have accomplished what you came for and you did your best, because you were here.

5

Wanting the World and Knowing Where You're At

I am no different from the average person. I am sure you have found yourself at a time in your life where you wanted to be somewhere you are not or wishing to be somewhere, but you didn't have the funds for it. I have too. As I have said before, patience hasn't been my friend. In fact, it has on too many occasions been my lesson.

When I decided I would write another book, I sat down and said to Rose:

"What am I going to write about because I am not that interesting."

"Write about your experiences," Rose replied. I immediately remembered my golden rule - everything happens in its own time, and when it is the right time. When we eventually pass away and go home, all we take with us are memories and experiences. We can't take any tangible things such as money, houses, cars or fame. What we experience now and in the moment is more important, because we are where we are supposed to be, in the here and now. If we are forever chasing our wants, we are not seeing what is in front of us or what is important in our lives. When you are chasing rainbows, so to speak, you may overlook the potholes in the road ahead of you, and therefore what might look like a hole in the road becomes a crater. If you happen to fall in that crater, it might be a long time before you manage to get out. I am not saying that we shouldn't follow our dreams or desires. Everyone needs to have something to strive towards. Realising just because we are not there yet, does not mean our dreams are not attainable, it just means we need to put in place a structure or foundations so that when we get there, our experiences will be memorable because we took the time to secure our foundations.

Wanting the world and knowing where I was at was an experience that I had in 2016-2017 and if I am honest, I am still there whilst I am writing this chapter. Although, heading into 2019, I had a greater understanding of what the title represents. Over the past two years, I have struggled to know what was right for me. I have many conversations with Darrin and Rose about what I need to do next regarding my career as a medium and realised my understanding of this, I could connect it to everyday life as a mother, daughter, friend and wife. I have always been worried about how other people saw me or if what I was doing in life was it the right thing. Up until a few years ago, I still thought this way. I was so focussed on other people's opinions that I lost sight of my own opinions, and my career wasn't my first concern. I was worried about whether I was a good mother, and if the values I was teaching my children were enough to get them through life. My greatest worry that was in the back of my mind:

"Have I done something wrong and scarred my children for life?" I sat down one day and said to myself:

"I'm tired." I became consciously aware I was thinking too much, to the point where my brain didn't want to function anymore because I was tired worrying about things that were out of my control. Instead of living in the moment, I was worrying about what might happen in the future. Effectively, instead of releasing my discomfort, I was creating a burden of anxiety, which I didn't need.

I believe that being in the moment means being in the present, and that life is a present. A present from God. Something that I was taking for granted, because I was more concerned about being perfect, I forgot about the present I was given when I was born - life. In 2017, my son graduated from high school and completed his Higher School Certificate - it was an emotional and stressful year. I had to juggle my career and being there for my children and husband. Like all parents, we all want our children to do well in their lives and I focused on my son's exams at the end of the year. Cameron has always been a bright boy, and on many occasions, his teachers have commented on this and it was a source of pride. I fell into the trap of expecting him to do well in the HSC, and this was reflected in the conversations we had.

In February of that year, I had a phone call from the school enquiring why Cameron's attitude to school had changed - some of his results reflected this. When I questioned him, he said that he was tired of school, and didn't want to be there anymore because he felt he was under too much pressure to perform well. Cameron has the same traits as me: worrying about other people's opinions and trying to be perfect. Darrin and I were worried, but we realised that we were expecting too much from our son. Because we were busy with life and our other commitments, we didn't see our son struggling. Cameron expressed his desire to leave school, and my first thought was about gaining the certificate first, because all of the hard work he had put in would be lost. We discussed this with him, and he decided to finish school because he only had six months to go. I have always had a good relationship with my son, however leading up the exams our connection was strained and consequently I felt like I was losing him.

To keep our connection, I decided to pull back and let him decide on his own path. I would be someone to talk to if he needed me, but the rest was up to him. I decided for my own health and sanity, I would stop worrying about the little things and accept them and move on. I kept saying to myself "it's not in my control, it's in his control." I had to let go of trying to control a situation I wasn't in charge of - I was trying to control my son's life and experiences. Our children have come down to earth with a contract to learn and experience their own lessons, not ours. But because I have had more life experience than my son, I felt it was the right thing to do - telling him what to do with his life, instead of moving to the side so he could experience life himself. I wanted to shield him from pain and getting hurt, and because I believed I knew best, I wasn't allowing him to grow as a soul and human being. It is natural for a parent to want to advise and to believe they are doing the best for their child. However, we must realise that life isn't always smooth travelling, there is going to be pitfalls and we will get muddy. But those muddy times that we experience will help define the person we are meant to be. It wasn't up to me to alter Cameron's contract that he arrived with, because he was the one who sat down with God and mapped out his life. The scars we obtain throughout our journey, whether they are emotional or physical, should be worn as reminders of where we came from, where we are now, and when it is time to go home. Our moments and memories we shared will last because they will be remembered in the physical world, and we will take them to heaven. I was reminded that being in the moment was more important than wanting to know the future.

6

Who Am I?

Who am I?
What makes me good enough?
Am I good enough to be put in front of people?
Am I worthy, of this gift from God?
Am I speaking the truth or saying the right information?
Am I really communicating with spirit or is it just my mind playing tricks?

These are the questions I that have asked myself hundreds of times throughout my career as a medium, and I still do. I have struggled many times over the years wondering if I was good enough to be the voice of spirit, and in the beginning when I realised that I had this gift, I questioned God.

"Why me?" I asked, as I believed I wasn't anything special, and I thought it was normal to speak to people who had crossed over. I would observe many people in various professions who I believed were successful in life such as film stars, doctors, lawyers, professional sports people and I even looked at royalty as a form of success. I realised that my belief of success was focused on people who were wealthy and were able to have the best things in life which meant they could afford lots of luxuries. As a child,

I knew that was what I wanted for myself and my family. My son only likes designer brands and considers having the best ones as his signature. Sometimes parents will dress their children in designer labels to show off their wealth. My dad always taught me to never to be jealous of someone else's success. *"You could be envious of them, but not to be jealous"*. This is something I live by, and I have taught that to my children, because jealousy or resentment is like a disease, and when you allow it to take hold of you, it embeds itself within you and can consume you. I have seen how resentment can consume a person in my own family, and instead of being happy for that person, they have become envious, nasty and suspicious for no reason. There was one person in my family, who, every time they saw me, they were distrustful of me because I was different. I believed they were fearful of the unknown. I was labelled the oddball. I am very different to my other family members and subsequently sometimes, people fear someone who is different. What I discovered, was that when a person is resentful, their expectations are high for everything. They expect things to be handed to them and life isn't going to give you answers on a silver platter.

Some people don't want to put the effort in, expecting others to do the work for them. We are here to live and learn, and sometimes, life throws us a curve ball, but it is what you do in that situation that is important. It is up to us to put the hard yards in, and whilst we are achieving our goals, our growth as a physical and spiritual person is always mounting. If people would stop and be who they are, and not worry about other people having more than them, there wouldn't be any jealousy or resentment in the world, because they would be content with what they have.

There are people in my life that believe being successful is measured by how much a person has in the bank, or the amount of properties they have. I am not saying people haven't worked hard for what they have, but I have also realised that it doesn't matter if you are wealthy or underprivileged - it matters if you are a good person and that goes a long way.

"My mum died the richest person I know, she didn't have a lot of money, but she had a lot of respect from people and this showed at her funeral because the congregation was massive," Rose said to me once. I am finding more and more these days that respect for other people or the environment is seriously lacking. No-one says hello or G'day anymore when they pass other people in the street or have common courtesy to say please or thank you. This is evident sometimes in my profession, people like to take from others, some people and it is a minor amount, believe that I am on tap twenty-four hours, seven days a week. That I will answer every call or read for people when they want a reading; I've even been asked to give a reading over the phone for no charge. I have been even offered double my fee to book people in ahead others who have booked over a year in advance. Money doesn't talk for me. I believe if I did this, not only am I being disrespectful towards the people who had booked first, but I am disrespecting spirit as well. I understand some people are desperate for a reading, and they believe they really need this, but ultimately it is up to spirit and our loved ones when they want to communicate with us. Others want guidance in their lives, but what I have learnt from this experience is that everything happens when it is meant to, if something is going to happen, it will and spirit or God, if you like, knows best.

I was talking to Rose one day and we were discussing success and how we defined success. Not surprisingly, we shared the same opinions. We both believed that having a house over our heads, food in the pantry, clothes on our backs, a bed to sleep in and waking up every morning is a blessing. I realised that most of us sit and worry about the things we don't have, and we never appreciate the things we do have. You may know the phrase - like attracts like - people with similar likes or who are very similar in personality who are placed on the same paths, and it isn't a coincidence their paths cross, because they are meant to meet.

Some people are meant to be in our lives for a moment, others are meant to stay forever, and others are meant to come in and out of our lives over time but are always there when we need them. The importance of this is for us as physical beings to learn something from these people. Whether it is a lesson, about how not to be or showing us a better way of doing things. Rose and I were meant to cross paths and it was amazing when I realised that we were so similar - the same, but different. I had finally found the person I could truly relate too and learn from.

I believe we have a physical mother who gave birth to us and who is here to teach us physical lessons, but we also have a spiritual mother who is here to help guide and educate us on our spiritual journey - Rose is my spiritual mother. Rose has been there when my spiritual journey needed a mother and she has, like a mother, given me a kick up the backside or chastised me when I needed it. Whilst we were talking, Rose said that when she was younger and wasn't doing this work professionally, she was experimenting with a reading for a man.

"Why don't you do this professionally and put yourself out there?" he continued to compliment her, telling her she should be doing this professionally, as she was very good at it. Rose, being young, thought

"No, who am I, I don't know a lot to do this work and I am not good enough. Who am I?" This resonated with me because I said the same thing when I first started my professional journey. Rose repeated what the man had told her:

"You're afraid of success and you don't realise how good you really are," and this was very true. I am afraid of success and ego, and I have given my family and friends permission to put me back in my place if my ego reveals itself. I know spirit will teach me a lesson as well. It hasn't been in my nature to put myself out there. I have always been happy to sit in the back of the room, and not crave the attention until recently. I was afraid people may have thought I was up myself, and I still struggle with advertising myself. That is why I have my husband Darrin to help with advertising. When a church asks me to talk about myself, it is usually brief, because I want to talk about what I love to do and that is to bring our love ones through. I will say that if spiritual people misuse or use their gift in a negative way, spirit will shut it down. The phone may stop ringing or people may stop attending readings. You will never lose your gift; however they will wait until you have learnt your lesson. Sometimes our lesson is to work on ourselves before we recommence spiritual work.

Sometimes you feel as though I am not worthy or good enough, but when you think about it, my knowledge and education has been going on for years. I started when I was five, and I could see and feel spirit. It was with me when I was born, and Rose was the same. It didn't start when I wanted to be a medium, it's been going on for years. People come into other people's lives for a reason, and their paths are destined to cross. Rose said that many years prior to our meeting, her nephew, who knew she was a reader, had talked about someone called Judy, who lived nearby, and she put her readings on a CD. As far as Rose was concerned, I was the only Judy in the area that did this. We were meant to meet. I remember the very first time I asked my Angels who was my guardian Angel and they said it was Rose.

Connections like the one I have with Rose, are ones that are meant to be made. This can go on for years until it is time to come together in one way or another, and spirit is very patient in that respect. As long, as you are being true to yourself and learning your lessons and developing in your own way, you are on the right track. Spirit's work isn't easy - it takes a lot of work, commitment, education, energy and it is hard at times. I have experienced times of exhaustion, and thinking that I am not good enough, or spirit is being too harsh. These are the times when I must assess where I am at. I have sat down and considered why I am feeling this way - most of the time it is self-inflicted because I have forgot the golden rule. When I am reading for another person, there is a trinity in progress. Not in the Catholic sense of Trinity (Father, Son and the Holy Ghost), to me this trinity is the information delivered from our loved ones, then to me and then to the person in front of me. The information isn't from me, it's from spirit through me. When I think I am not good enough, I am really making this about myself and not about spirit. In my experience, spirit will always be in control of how the reading progresses, and if I make it about me, then they hang up the phone or wait until the right time. I have discovered that when you doubt yourself, it is time to be in the moment, take a breath, relax and this helps to clear the mind because if my head was full of other information before I started my work, how can our loved ones get through to communicate.

I was in my pity-party mood recently, and a friend said:

"God gave you this gift for a reason, and every time you doubt yourself, you are doubting him and effectively slapping him in the face, figuratively speaking." I must admit that comment was my wakeup call. I am not saying I am the Chosen One, because I'm not. Accept who you are, and don't worry about what other people are doing, because chances are there will always be people who are better at something than you are. We will never know who the best medium in the world is, because they are doing the work and not advertising how good they are. I understand that it doesn't matter if a person has gotten the where I want to be: all that matters is that I know if it is meant to be, then it will be and when the time is right, spirit will show me the way because I will be more prepared to tackle whatever I have to face. The story of the three little pigs is one that I like to associate with to my spiritual journey, or you could relate it to a part of your life. The first pig made his house out of straw, the second pig made it out of wood and the last pig made it out of brick. In the story the two pigs who made their houses out of straw and wood finished their houses quicker than the third pig, but they didn't last. However, the third pig who made his house out of brick, took longer, but his house lasted. Some people may have gotten to where they are or to the top quicker than you, but if you take your time your efforts are more structured and sturdier.

A person's race to the top may be quick, but they haven't put in the work and secured their foundations and what they have worked towards may fall. Consequently, the person who has taken their time would be doing the work a lot longer but have a different result. It's all about knowing that success doesn't happen overnight, and that long-lasting success must be worked at, day in, day out, year in, year out. The people who get there quickly - where are they in ten years' time? I want to be doing this work for a long time, not a short time. As long as we believe in ourselves, and complete our tasks to the best of our ability, that is all that matters.

7

Taking Responsibility

My dad's favourite saying whilst I was growing up was - "I would like to wake up in a hundred years and see how the world has changed." As the years go by, I am thinking of this saying more and more these days, especially doing the work I do. This saying has become important during my time as a medium. I know life changes all the time, and according to evolution, we need changes to happen to help us grow as physical beings, whether it is a good change or a bad change. These changes create experiences, skills and knowledge.

I have noticed these days that most people don't take their responsibilities seriously. Nor do they believe they are responsible for their own actions. I believe people often think that something is someone else's problem repeatedly, and not theirs. They blame everyone else for these problems. People can be quick to judge others without taking a good look in the mirror at themselves. It is easy to blame others without knowing all the facts. I myself have not been exempt from this. My eldest daughter has frequently pulled me up on my own actions and judgements. Although at the time I believed I wasn't judging the situation or a person, on reflection I actually was, and my daughter was right. I am sure you have seen this happen or done it yourself.

"Who was the one who didn't close the front door when they came in?" Our parents would ask us. Instead of owning up to this, it was easier to blame our siblings or even the dog, as in my case. I have found it is easier to say that something wasn't my fault rather than owning up. Of course, there are two sides to every story, and you need all the facts before deciding. Sometimes, as physical beings, we don't own our actions, and we don't walk the walk or talk the talk.

What I have been taught both by spirit and by Rose is that we are the only ones that have control over our actions, and taking responsibility is taking charge of ourselves. It is not up to anyone else to tell us what to do in the physical world, and it is our choice whether we allow other people to take control of us. There will always be situations that are out of our control, but I am talking about people taking control of their own actions. I use this analogy in my readings: "If you fall down tomorrow, I will be there to help pick you up, but it will be your legs that will help you stand." The only person that can be held accountable for what you do is yourself. It is not up to us to blame anyone else if something isn't right in our lives. If something isn't going your way or you don't like something, the only person who can change the situation is yourself. For many years, I have been worried about my weight, and being a dancer, my weight and body image has always been important to me. However, after I had my third child, my body image changed. When I underwent treatment due to a thyroid condition and after my hysterectomy four years ago, my weight became an issue, and it has been harder to maintain. I have for many years, made negative comments about my body. I should be grateful for what I have. At times, I do feel a little selfish because my body is working well without any major concerns, but I still don't like the way I look. My body is mine to take care of and if I want to change my body image, it is up to me. I could sit in a corner and ask:

"Why was I born this way?" and not do anything about it, or I can get off my backside, and make the necessary changes

I need or want. This means eating healthy food and exercising and accepting that who I am is important. I realised that I am not going to be in my twenties anymore and after having three children, my body will never be the same again. Accepting who I am is the first step in taking responsibility of who I am and my life.

How many times have you taken the easy option to get out of things? I have when it comes to dieting and not eating sugar. It is so easy to say I will start tomorrow, or we find excuses like I'm tired or I haven't got enough time. Many times, I have been impatient, and wanted a quick fix like taking a pill and remarkably everything will be fixed. We as society have become lazy and want others to do the work for us without looking at our lives and making the necessary changes on our own. It is so easy to get other people to mow our lawns, clean our houses, tutor our children, handymen to fix things around the house or order groceries online because our lives have become so busy and time-consuming, that we don't make time to do these things. I often hear myself telling my children that I am busy, and I remember my mum saying the same thing when I was a child. I am not saying that we are not busy and have things to do, but it is my responsibility to take the time to listen to my children, and give them the time they need because in a blink of an eye they will be grown up and won't have the time to converse with me and I know I will wonder where the time has gone.

As a mother, I have the responsibility as a parent to teach my children the difference between right and wrong, to have respect for others and to help guide them through their challenges in life. Nevertheless, it is their responsibility to work with what they have been taught, and their actions will have consequences. You cannot blame another person for your actions, because at the end of the day, you have made that choice even if someone else suggested it. My mum's favourite saying as we were growing up was:

"If your friend wanted to jump off the Harbour Bridge, would you?" In other words - if another person wanted to do something even if they knew the consequences were going to be bad, would you follow them.

There are two sides to every story. In my readings with clients, I read from the heart, and my connection with spirit is from the heart. Therefore, the connection with my client is from the heart. I read a quote the other day and it was a little boy touching a wall closing his eyes:

"Share with your heart." This resonated with me because it is so true. Being responsible for our own actions means that we need to listen with our heart and cherish our soul. When is the last time you the reader have asked your soul what you need to know?

In 2018, I was experiencing a lot of energy changes in my life, and to be honest, these were energies that I had not experienced before. I felt overwhelmed, confused, I couldn't focus, I didn't feel I was good enough, my mind wouldn't settle down and I was overthinking things too much. I was also picking up on everyone and their energy and their ailments. I was feeling like I was going crazy. I spoke to the one person I trust, and I knew they would guide me on the right path, and not give me the answers but help me to understand what I needed to know. Rose told me that whenever you feel like this again, sit down and ask your spirit what it needs. It was so simple, I thought, but true. I was feeling frustrated for weeks, not knowing or understanding why I had felt this way. The remedy was as simple as to go back to the essence that is me - my soul and what I could do to help the energy shift. If you ever feel as though you are in this situation, instead of trying to find answers in the future, and are getting frustrated because the answers may not be there, go back to the beginning, your soul, or the basics. Your soul or intuition will never steer you wrong, whether you ask it a question, or it comes from a feeling. It is always right even if you don't like what it is telling you. Your soul is the purest part of you, and it is connected to the divine, and their messages will always speak the truth. I did sit down and ask my soul what I needed to know regarding my energy. I didn't receive the answer straight away, but I recognised the words I was getting for weeks, and it was fun. My soul said for me to go and have some fun. I began to understand that my soul tells me exactly what to do and where to do it, I was given one word...fun and it was up to me to carry out this request. I have learnt by connecting to your soul means connecting to your true self and it is your responsibility to listen to your soul and to know what the best path is for you.

8

Accountability

In 2018, I along with many other people, felt the energy around the world dramatically shift. It felt as though it was quite negative, depressing, soul crushing and at times suffocating. Where I live in Sydney Australia the weather was scorching in the high thirty to forty degrees Celsius, which didn't help at all. I felt as though my energy was being sucked from me and I had doubts about my work, it began to play on my mind on a regular basis.

I knew something was happening in the universe, and consequently the world was beginning to change. I remember seeing a live feed once through Hay House about Sharman Workers in Peru and their prophecies about the world. Sharmic Medicine filmed a Sharman reading, and the Sharman said Mother Earth is not very happy with humanity because of the way we have been taking from her for centuries. Even though the Sharman did not directly say humanity was the cause of the catastrophes over the years, it got me thinking about accountability.

The Sharman said that Mother Earth may not mend fully because of our actions, but she knows there are people trying to help minimise the damage we are doing. It is not my intention to get on my soapbox and preach that the world needs to change because I am not an authority. I'm just a normal person who is trying to work through the lessons in her life and trying to understand and work through the energy shifts that affect me.

During a reading one day, spirit helped me to understand a little about what was going on in the world. I was told the energy in the world is negative because of people's fear. Many people feared what was going to happen next, or they were uncertain about the future. The news was filled with reports of aggressive behaviour from current world leaders.

This got me thinking about Quality verses Quantity, some companies were only interested in making money and the workers who helped make this money were pushed aside. They were given more deadlines and stress, and this caused worry and ultimately, a sense of fear. To help us counteract this negativity and stabilise the energy around us, spirit asked me to be more positive. How many times have you looked at a negative situation or responded negatively first? I realised that in the past and because of this energy shift, I was being lazy, and my attitude and actions had been unenthusiastic. I was allowing the negative energy to control me. My own actions were affecting my family environment as well. It was easy for me to say what the hell. Or to think or act negatively before I sat down and evaluated the situation and saw the positive side. People are so quick to judge others or blame each other without realising that they might be accountable for the negativity.

So, I listened to spirit, and every day they said to find a positive thing and say it out loud and let it go. Say one word or a phrase that is positive about the day, yourselves or others. Humanity has put so much harmful energy into the world, it is up to us to neutralise it with positivity. Electricity always has a positive, and a negative for it to work. We human beings need to be accountable for our own actions and thoughts for this energy to improve.

When you were young, it was easy to blame another person or situation when we were in trouble. We didn't want to face the consequences of our own actions, so we deflected the blame somewhere else. My children have been great deflection ambassadors, and I am sure my parents would argue I did the same thing.

In 2018, I was experiencing the terrible teenage years, my daughter had turned fifteen the previous year, and she went from a loving, caring and non-argumentative young girl to a challenging and argumentative young lady. This was a trying time, resulting in, at times, a less productive environment for the family. Our relationship was tense, and we argued frequently. It was a very trying time, and I often found myself questioning my parenting and where I went wrong. I would never have spoken to my parents that way. People would tell me it was just the age, and she would get over it. But when you are living through it, it is tough to know what mood she would be in when she arrived home from school or when she woke up every day. It was like walking on eggshells, and I loathed feeling like this. It didn't help that my daughter was experiencing hormonal changes, and I was going through menopause.

When I sat down to write this chapter, I realised that I was accountable for my own actions. Instead of sitting down and trying to find a solution to work through what I was experiencing, I was pessimistic and blamed my daughter's behaviour on hormones. It was easy for me to see the negative.

My star sign is Cancer, so building a wall around myself or retreating from life would be the first thing I would do, and that is exactly what I did.

Many of my friends would say you need to be the adult, and sometimes I didn't feel like being the adult. But being the adult means recognising when to retreat from an unproductive situation, or to get out of my own space and see things in a new perspective. This is exactly what I did: I had to get out of my own space and see the real issue. I focused on how I felt during situations that made me feel anxious. I realised my expectations I have of myself are the same expectations I have for my children.

I am a perfectionist and put 100 per cent in all that I do, and I expect the same behaviour from my children, whether it is right for them or not.

"You can't put an old head on a young man's shoulders," my dad would often tell me. The meaning behind this was: you can't tell young people how things were done in your day and expect them to do it the same way. Being older may not make you wiser but the experience's and knowledge we gain in life help to build our souls development and navigate our journey through life.

There are situations in our lives that are out of our control, but it is what you do in that situation that is important. We will always get through something, but it is entirely up to us: we can sit down and give up or we can wake up every day and put our best foot forward. As a medium, I am accountable for my own actions, even though it is spirit talking through me. How I present the information is important. For instance, if spirit told me to tell a client to stop being negative, how I present this information to the person is important, so I don't come across as being negative or judgemental. I must be aware that spirit might say it in an encouraging way, and it is my responsibility to deliver the information correctly to that person because I am accountable in the representation of spirit. Owning your words is important, I always tell my clients. I give you what I get - and that means I give the information spirit gives me to my clients without judgement. If I have misinterpreted information spirit has given me, I can't just turn around and say that is spirit's fault because they were the ones who gave me the information first.

We as physical beings are always accountable for our actions and voices. We can't blame others or situations for our own mistakes. Even if circumstances are out of our control, it is the way we handle things that is important, because the journey helps us to understand our future endeavours, good or bad. At the end of the day, I reached the conclusion that my daughter and I were too much alike and we both were stubborn, perfectionist and independent - and I must work through strategies that will help benefit us.

9

Respectful Behaviour

I was compelled to write about respectful behaviour after something I experienced in a supermarket and suffice to say, I believe I didn't do anything wrong.

It happened one night I when was picking my son up from work. Before I went home, I sent him to the car whilst I went to the supermarket to buy groceries. When I finished shopping, I was waiting in the queue. A woman was moving her trolley forwards, and as she did, a bottle of drink fell on the floor. Her family were in front of her, processing their groceries. I watched in disbelief as the woman just walked away and left the spillage on the floor and did not notify an attendant from the store. She then proceeded to put her empty container in a carrying basket and not in the garbage a few feet from the store. I was speechless!

Beside me, there was another customer, who also saw the incident. This customer informed the checkout attendant, and the family of this lady about the spillages. The family just looked at the customer behind them and ignored the comments. Luckily, another attendant came and cleaned the floor. It was my turn to go through the checkout, and I was telling the checkout attendant a personal story of how my best friend was shopping in a supermarket, and someone had spilled a drink and didn't notify anyone (just the same as this person), and my friend slipped on the floor. As a result of someone else's carelessness, she had to have knee surgery.

Whist I was talking to the attendant, the lady and her family came back and spoke aggressively to me. They assumed I was being disrespectful towards their mother. I tried to explain that I wasn't talking about her negatively, but they didn't listen and all they said that I should respect their mother. I was astounded.

"Your mother should respect other people and notify someone if she spills liquid." The mother wasn't that old, and I believe she should know better. She was embarrassed, because she was caught being disrespectful. I wasn't the person who notified the family or attendant when it happened, but because I was alone, the family decided to attack me. They didn't take responsibility for her actions, and didn't believe she was accountable, even though their mother was the one who was in the wrong. I believe the family were playing the you must respect your elders' card. Let me get one thing clear: I am always respectful to my elders. This is what I was taught by my parents and what I have taught my children. However, it is very hard to respect another person, who blatantly knows what they have done, and doesn't respect others around them, for example leaving liquid on the floor and not preventing an accident.

When I was a nurse, I taught my students to treat a patient, the way you would like to be treated, and I believe in the golden rule - do unto others as you would have them do unto you. I have come to realise that there are individuals in our society that do not practise this, and it is disappointing. If we do not apply the golden rule, it will be lost for future generations and society may become more self-absorbed and respectful behaviour may be non-existent. My personal story is a simple daily example of how an individual should be accountable for their actions. If a person demands respect, I believe respect must be earned in the first place. When you have respect for yourself, you will have respect for others.

10

Something Worth Pondering

Every day, we as physical beings are presented with opportunities to learn. The difference between the individual who learns, and the individual who doesn't is: the person who wants to learn is gaining an acceptance of knowledge and embracing new opportunities in their lives. Sometimes our lives may not go according to plan. It might not be the right time for what we want to do. My niece wanted to move from one state to another, and she believed she would get a job quickly because she was young. This wasn't the case for her at the time. She had applied for numerous jobs, had numerous interviews, and nothing came of any. One of the jobs she applied for took three weeks to receive any sort of reply. The endless waiting was difficult for a young person, but whilst she was waiting for the company to get back to her, she was offered another position with another company, which suited her. Sometimes, when we expect things to happen in our way, and they don't, we get up tight and believe the world is out to get us. But if we take a step back, and be accountable for our own actions, we realise that if something doesn't happen in our time frame, it doesn't mean it won't happen. There is always something better or more suited for us in the future. I have overreacted many times and I have learnt, if something doesn't go my way, I don't yell and scream why me. I sit and say:

"I let go and let God" and give it to my Angels and God and wait for when it is the right time for me to receive.

11

Judgement

Judge not, that you be not judged.
Matthew 7:1

Before I sat down to write this chapter, I was hearing the word judgement in my mind. I wasn't sure what it meant at first, but after watching a movie one weekend that had a profound impact on me, I realised what God was trying to tell me. The movie talked about judgement, and how humanity is quick to judge someone because of their race, colour, the way they wear their hair or someone's profession without knowing that individual personally.

It got me thinking about my own personal experience I had with my aunty who was also my godmother. I decided to write down my story, but before I started, I looked to heaven, and asked for her permission to include this in my book. My aunty died a couple a years ago. I asked for a sign whilst hanging out the washing. It was an overcast day, and there were plenty of black clouds in the sky. It had been raining the night before, and I went to hang out cushions from my deck. As I was doing this, some amazing sunlight peered through black clouds out of nowhere. I knew this was my sign and when I was walking back inside, I found a single feather on my mat at the doorway. I looked up to heaven, and thanked my aunty, and said to my Angels:

"Let's go, we have work to do". I went into my reading room, where I never write because I consider this my working environment. This time, I started to write. I was told this was where they wanted me to write today, and I have learnt, you never question your Angels.

This story started a few years ago, when my mum visited my aunty and uncle for my uncle's seventieth birthday. All the family had been invited to the party, but unfortunately, I couldn't make it due to other family commitments. A few days before my mum and dad were due to leave for the party, my grandfather's spirit came to see me. He had a message for the birthday boy, along with the other family members, because all his children would be in the one place. I was so excited, and I told my mum the message. Unfortunately, she couldn't give the message to everyone at the party, because there wasn't enough time, so she decided to leave the message for my aunty for another time. Mum called my aunty a few days after the party and during the conversation she tried to relay the message my grandfather gave. At that point my aunty stopped the conversation.

"I do not believe in that stuff and Judy is an embarrassment to the family." My mum was speechless and ended the conversation quickly. The next day mum called me and told me what happened with my aunty and what was said. I was speechless, and emotional. I was hurt, angry, disillusioned and felt rejected. I have always been different to my family members, but these comments coming from my godmother really hurt. Once I got over my initial shock and anger, not to mention a few choice words I might have said in retaliation, I said to my mum:

"How can she say that? She doesn't even know me or seen the work that I do."

I need to clarify something: I had not seen my aunty in several years. My aunty was also a minister's wife, and therefore her religious beliefs didn't allow for her to see the work I do kindly. She was very much a believer in God and Jesus. So am I. It amazes me when I have people who come and see me, they ask:

"So are you Catholic, and do you believe in God?" because of the work I do. My answer is always the same:

"I was christened Church of England and of course I believe in God. I thank God every day for my beautiful gift, and the spirits and the wonderful people I meet along the way. I was born with this gift from God and I cherish is every day."

"Let it go and don't worry about it," my mum said. But I was having a hard time accepting what my aunty said. It was like I needed validation from my family for the work I do.

A few months later, my mum called to say that my aunty was diagnosed with an incurable disease called Motor Neurone Disease. I felt incredibly sorry for her and her family, because I knew what the disease was from my years working as a nurse, and Darrin's grandmother also died of this disease a few years before I met him. My aunt's health declined over the next two years. After this decline, she passed away. I remember performing at an event prior to this and my grandfather came through with a message for my dad. He said:

"My aunty will last until Christmas and I will be there to greet her," and this is exactly what happened. Before she passed on, I wrote a letter to her, just to let her know I was thinking of her. On the day of her funeral, the minister who was close to my aunt's family discussed my aunt's life and how she gave her time and energy to many people in the church that my uncle was a minister at. A lot of people were very grateful and cherished my aunt's kindness and dedication. I realised just as much my aunty didn't know about the work I do, that I didn't know about the work she had done. As the minister recapped my aunt's life story, I was interested in one aspect: her dedication to Jesus. I recognised we both shared the same dedication and faith in Jesus, and this was evident in the work we both did. We just practised different methods. We were the only people who went into the nursing profession in our family as well.

The day after the funeral I had my first sign from my Aunty, I was driving my son to work, and it was around Christmas time. I was driving towards a roundabout and as I was stopped, I saw a man walking across the road in front of my car carrying a gigantic cross. He looked like Jesus carrying the cross before he was crucified. I was stunned, and I had to look twice to believe what I was seeing. I even asked Cameron if he was seeing the same thing. To justify this, I thought to myself:

"This is Christmas, and of course a man is carrying an enormous cross across the road in front of me." I told my friend what had happened, and she said:

"Wasn't Jesus crucified on the cross at Easter?"

The second sign came a week later, when I was reading for one of my clients. A loved one was coming through who had passed away with the Motor Neurone Disease. I also felt my aunt's presence.

"I am sorry." I was thankful to hear those words, but a small part of me wondered if I was wanting this so much, that I may have imagined this. My aunty died in the December, and in the January, I had this feeling I needed to have a reading with a friend of mine. She is a great reader, and we are very similar. I was urged to call her, and I did. The reading got started and she said that she'd had Jesus and the Holy Spirit here before I came which was comforting. She went on to say I have a message from your aunty. I was shocked because my friend didn't know my story regarding my aunty and our relationship or what was said. She said before you came today, I wrote down what she wanted to tell you, and this is what was said:

"Sometimes I still don't believe what Judy does.

I've spoken to them - Jesus and Mary and it's true.
She is real, and she is amazing! The real deal!

Sorry love, to treat you like I did. I'm really sorry.

I'm on your side!

I know for sure you are an Earth Angel, and yes, we don't die. We just move interstate and change postcodes.

I love you Judy!"

After reading what my aunty said, I just cried. From that day I let go of the hurt I had carried from what my aunty had said years ago, and I recognised judgement. It is so easy to judge something or someone without having all the facts. It's even harder to let go of something we need too so we can move forward in our lives. Most of the time we can't forgive a person because we don't want to forgive them. Forgiveness is the first stage of letting go. You may be angry still, and it might take a thousand times to say I forgive you before it is gone. If the intent of forgiveness is in your heart, you will get there: it just takes time.

The lesson I learnt from my experience, was that my aunty and I were similar in some ways, but different in others. We both loved meeting people and helping them and this made an impact. My profession allows me to meet wonderful people and amazing spirits and the joy is how I can give back and help people to receive peace in knowing their loved ones are okay and happy in heaven….it is truly a gift from God.

12

What's the Old saying? Patience is a Virtue

To understand patience, I asked my husband Darrin to write about his experiences in this area, the following paragraphs are his beliefs surrounding patience.

The hardest lesson to learn in life is patience. It is human nature to want everything when we want it. People sometimes find themselves battling their current situation instead of accepting it. In my experience, too many people focus on what they want to achieve and not why they want to achieve it. Therefore, nothing happens when they expect it to. If the why is rock solid, then it will happen within a reasonable timeframe.

When most people hear the word patience, they immediately think that means they have to wait longer than they want to. This doesn't have to be the case at all. If you can display patience, then you continue to work towards your goal. One of my favourite sayings is:

"Everything happens in Gods time." I learnt that this has more truth to it than I wanted to accept. For years I have been in the wrong jobs and I was always forced to change my career. I got into the habit of expecting something to happen to make me change my career at the time. I didn't take a step back and look at what I had and what I really wanted to do with my life. We all get very comfortable with what we know and limit our comfort zone to what is considered acceptable.

It was only when I took time to reflect on my life that I realised I had missed the point altogether. Each job I have had has taught me a valuable lesson that led me to discover my life's purpose. My purpose was to help people. You have no idea how exciting it was to finally realise that my entire life had been dedicated to helping others. I decided to take on Life Coaching and make it official that I was now actively and consciously helping people with issues that arose in their lives. This was also at a time in my life where my family was devastated by four close relatives passing away in the same year. My grandfather was one of these people, and what he left me was the answer to what my life's purpose is. He left me some money which I immediately invested into my Life Coach training. He had awoken the person that I wanted to be with all my heart and soul. I will be forever grateful to my grandfather for what he did for me.

When you think about when things happen and why, the answer isn't always clear. That is when you must take a step back, compose yourself and look at things from the outside. It's not easy to be objective about yourself but when you are, you will finally accept patience. For me, my grandfather's passing was the right time for me to start studying again, as he gave me the means to do it. You are never too old to start something new. If you are struggling to accept this, then it's only because that is the way you have conditioned yourself. Everyone experiences a makeover at least once in their lives, when out with the old, in with the new comes into play. We should all be looking at what makes us who we are and assessing if your current beliefs are a part of your current goals.

The phrase that I have always held close is: you are where you need to be right now. I love this because it reassures us that no matter what may be going on in your life, you need to experience

THE VOICE OF SPIRIT: THE WORLD THROUGH MY EYES

it to become the person you want to be. Having said this, is it okay to just exist and not look for your life's purpose? I think so. You may already be living the life that you are comfortable with. Your success in life is not measured by the amount of money you have in the bank but by the impact you have on other people's lives.

Over the years, I have realised helping people feel at peace is very important in my profession. It is what I am driven to do. The best compliment I can receive from a client, whether it is through email or word of mouth is that they're at peace now. When that happens, I look to the heavens and say a huge thank you to spirit. It means the world to me when a person feels complete and can look forward to a future knowing their loved ones are happy and watching over them daily. I was once told by Rose:

"You never know the impact you have made on a person.".
I love what I do, and I thank God every day for my gift and the beautiful people I meet. I don't do this work for the compliments or the accolades because without spirit, I wouldn't be me or have this gift.

Although helping others and giving them peace is a major reason why I do what do. I am also aware I am not here to fix things for others. Many times, I have said:

"I am not here to dot the I's or cross the T's." That is up to the person sitting in front of me. My purpose is to be the voice of spirit and give people the information I receive. I give what I get, even though I don't always understand the information I receive, but most of the time my client does. I was giving a reading to client on day and their relative said to mention a pig. At the time, I thought it was quite weird and I thought my client would think I was crazy, but of course I said pig, and the client cracked up laughing. They used to have a pig who was part of the family, and their husband loved that pig. I always love it (not) when spirit puts me in it. This also happens when I am told to call a person by a certain name, of course I think this is a nickname. But it is always uncomfortable when I mention the name, and a client says they hated the name. The moral of the story is that spirit loves to play tricks on you! I always see spirit either laughing at me or have a cheesy grin on their face when this happens.

Like most of us, patience is one of my major lessons in life. I can honestly say I do not like the word, and it is hard for me to have patience. I am getting a lot better at it as I am getting older but is still hard when you want what you want in life.

There have been many times spirit has taught me a lesson about patience, and this goes hand in hand with having faith. Many times, I have called Rose and she has listened to me babbling about how I must wait for things while I ask when my turn will be. I know she is on the other end of the phone smiling and will reply it will happen in God's time. This is a phrase I have become very familiar with, and even my husband Darrin says it to me now.

We are all human, and we live in a physical world. Everything is at our fingertips. Everything is on demand - we no longer have to wait for anything. If you want to watch a movie, you no longer go to Blockbuster. You just download it from Foxtel or Netflix. When I was a child, I never had a television in my room and no Foxtel. If a movie came out in the cinemas, I would have to wait to see or wait until it came to the video store and when the movie did arrive, I would have to wait longer because it would be already hired. Thanks to technology, everything is accessible. We don't have to go out to the shops anymore if we don't want to, because we can order our groceries and clothes online and they are delivered the next day or in a week. Consequently, we put unrealistic expectations on ourselves and others. People will come and see me and only want one person to come through. This becomes difficult if I can see a grandmother, and all the person wants is their father to be standing beside them. It is not to say that the person isn't there, it is because the grandmother has a stronger energy and is in my face.

It is a first in, best dressed scenario sometimes. Most of the time, once I have acknowledged one person, they open the door to the person the client was hoping to talk too. I am learning to be patient every day. I try to perfect what I know, but it is not easy. I have a lifetime to do it. Like most people I have a bucket list. One thing on my list is going to Scotland, where my ancestors come from and hopefully perform on platform. This is my dream, and spirit has shown me signs that I am going there, but not when. One thing I do know, spirit doesn't give a timeline. In 2013, during a reading with a client, they mentioned they had purchased a small piece of land in Scotland. They had done it because people had been encouraged to purchase small bits of land so that the land would not be developed by property developers because of its natural beauty. I got onto the Internet and purchased two plots for my dad and myself. A few weeks later, Darrin received an email from the same organisation saying we had been given a third plot for free. I have had clients who came for a reading, and at the time I didn't know they were coming because they had taken the spot of another person and when I met them, they were Scottish or they had just returned from visiting relatives in Scotland.

13

Spirit Always Knows Best

Do you believe that our lives are mapped out for us or that there is a higher power looking out for us that ultimately knows best? This is a question I have been asked by many people, including my family. I have always said *"it doesn't matter what another person believes in, it is what you believe that is the most important thing, and your experiences are yours and yours alone"*. We are only here in the physical for our soul to grow, and we learn through these experiences and decisions we make. Some people have to make difficult decisions about their family members going into a care facility. Even though it is hard decision, it is done with their best interests at heart. This is the case with spirit. You may have heard the saying God only gives you what you can handle - and even at the time it might feel you are being victimised or that God hates you. In the long run, he or a higher power knows you can handle it and get through it. I believe that everyone will always get through their challenges. We choose whether to refuse to move forward or accept where we are in life. Even if we take one day at a time, we are still making progress forward, it may not be as fast or slow as we want but it is still moving. In the long run, spirit always knows best. I have always said to my children and clients -"" *a mistake is only a mistake if we do not learn from it.* I explain this through an analogy:

"If you fall down tomorrow, I would hold my hand out and help you up, but it would be your legs that would hold you." Unless you have a physical disability that prevents you to stand, no-one else will stand for you. I have noticed many people always have something to say whether they should or not. Everyone is so quick to judge or put their two bobs worth in as my grandfather always said. I learnt this long ago when I was criticised by my aunty for being a medium. There are some instances that advice given is warranted, but it is also important to know that before you give advice, just be mindful of the consequences that this advice might have or that some people may not be ready to hear it even though you believe they should know. The reason I go to spiritual church is to learn. I like watching various mediums and learning from them and this includes listening to their teachings and its always great to resonate with them. This was the case with a well-respected and wonderful medium named Sylvia. I don't always have the time to go to church, but when I need to, spirit will always make it happen. Traditionally, when a medium is performing a reading at church, they do an address before they start their readings. The best ones I have found are the talks that are educational, and this was the case with Sylvia's address. She talked about being held accountable as a medium and this meant, be mindful of what you say to people. There have been situations in my professional career where spirit has given me information and I have had to consider that this information may not be in the best interest to give to my client. Spirit may have said to a reader that someone's partner is having an affair and you the reader blurt out what spirit said without thinking of the consequences especially if the client didn't even know their partner was cheating. Even though spirit gave the medium the information, how you deliver it matters. Do you say something and hope for the best or do you acknowledge spirit and let the person find out for themselves, in case we have misinterpreted the message from spirit? They may have said there was a someone cheating but they may not specify who it is, and your actions may have dramatic consequences. As a medium, I do receive information from spirit, and I know that the information I receive is not mine to give. Why does spirit give me that information in the first place and they told me once - because they can!

One of the first things I explain to a client in a reading is that I do not give bad information unless I am pushed to give it. If spirit wanted me to tell the client, they would make it happen. Of course, in the past when I have been given the information and I am not sure of it, I will question spirit and they will either say it's up to me to decide or push me to do so. Sylvia spoke about actions and consequences and knowing the difference between spirits voice and our own voice which leads to our own judgements or opinions. In my experience, my opinion about something doesn't matter and some things are best left unsaid.

Most times when I am communicating with spirit my client, I don't remember what I have said because I am the go-between, and the words just come out. This was the case with two people: one was at an event I held, and another was in a private reading. In both cases, I was shocked, and they were classic examples of spirit wanting their loved one to know something, and how they will make it happen if they want us to know.

I was doing a platform event in August 2017, and at that event I spoke to a woman regarding her mother-in-law. During that reading I spoke about someone having a stroke. Four days later, I received a message from a lady from the night telling me that on the night I gave her a reading, her mother-in-law had a massive stroke. I was speechless at the time of reading and the message because I didn't remember the message and it was out of the ordinary for me. All I could think to say, was sorry and ask if the family was okay. I had to sit down and digest the information and realised it was the message spirit gave me prior to the night. They said that I needed to trust that the information would be given to me when I needed it, and that they would be in control. Before every reading or event, I do get quite nervous. As you can imagine, standing in front of a crowd can be very nerve-racking.

I pray to every Angel and being and the Ascended Master to help me see and hear spirit clearly. It can also be overwhelming because you know that there are a lot of people who would dearly love to speak to their loved ones. In the beginning, I was nervous that spirit wouldn't turn up, and I would then be standing there with nothing. Thankfully, this has not been the case. I have recently been given a good lesson. I was told once that the spirit world and my Angels will never let you down if you come from the right space or light. I was told I had to believe this, and I did to an extent. There was still a part of me that had to accept it and let go. To truly trust spirit is to let go of your insecurities. You can be nervous, but spirit will never let you down and will always know best.

It was three days until my event, and this was exciting because I had started to spread my wings, and this was a new venue and place. That week I had my clients whom I saw one-on-one and on Thursday of that week, my voice went - there was no reason for it. I thought it would be okay, because I didn't need it again until Saturday night. However, by Saturday morning after sucking on lozenges, drinking honey and lemon tea, and gargling with warm salty water, my voice was still absent I was a little panicked that it wouldn't return. I sat down and asked the question why to spirit. They didn't answer straight away, but when they did, I heard it loud and clear.

"It is not up to you to give messages to the people; you are our voice and you need to trust that we will not let you down. You have to have faith that we will support you." It wasn't until an hour before the event that my voice was recognisable. It was a lesson in faith and belief.

Our loved ones are not always specific in their messages. This happens quite often. It is not my job to decipher what spirit is trying to say. It is my job to be their voice, and it is up the person sitting in front of me to interpret it. This was the case with a lady who came to see me in September 2017. She wrote a message on my members-only page that she had come for a reading six months ago, and at the start of her session I said:

"Can I be completely honest with you?" She said yes. The first thing spirit had to say was that her grandmother had either passed or was preparing to pass, I continued to say -

"Her grandmother was sitting next to her with her arm draped around her, and her grandfather in spirit said it was time and she needed to come with him." I relayed that her grandmothers' spirit was preparing to cross over (her grandmother was still alive) but, her soul was getting to start the transition into heaven because she was sleeping longer hours.

My client never forgot the message, and unfortunately, she would feel sick when the phone would ring with calls from family members - as she thought they were calling to give her bad news. She had two grandmothers living, and the one thing spirit did not say was which grandmother they were talking about. One morning this lady woke up to and was doing various errands with her son. She told her father that he could enjoy the morning to himself. As my client was walking out the door, she noticed a message for her father from her aunty asking him to get in touch with her immediately. Her father's mother was in hospital and her condition overnight had taken a turn for the worse. Her dad left immediately to be with his mum. The penny had dropped regarding her reading, and it dawned on her that the whole time she was waiting for her mum's mum to pass that she completely forgot about her dad's mum. During her reading, Spirit would often refer to the coast, and she hadn't made the connection her dad's mum lived on the coast. Her grandmother passed peacefully, surrounded by her loving family. The reading gave comfort to her whole family at a time of extreme sadness. To say I was blown away by the message would be an understatement. I now understood that even if you think you know something, spirit always knows best and they are completely in control of how the messages are delivered and the outcomes. It was a privilege to be spirit's voice and to give comfort to my client, knowing her grandmother was ready and surrounded by love before she passed was amazing.

14

Spirit is in Control

Not listening to your intuition or ignoring spiritual messages has consequences in life and from spirit. I have, on many occasions, been in this situation and the end result is always the same: spirit is in control and knows what's best for me. Over the years, I have been slapped with the proverbial bat many times, and now I have learnt that the spiritual message will be revealed in its own time. It doesn't matter when you get the information or how long it takes, as long as you get it. There have been many times in my life when I haven't understood what spirit was trying to tell me or I have been impatient about knowing what the next step is for me. Every time I have tried to force the issue, spirit has always known best and has made me wait and be patient. If I have been impatient, and didn't listen, then I have learnt a lesson. Most of the time the thing I wanted turned out to be what I didn't want in the first place. It's like the saying the grass is always greener on the other side, but sometimes there can be bindies.

I believe that our lives are mapped out for us before we are born, and we have made a contract with God. During this time, our lessons and experiences are mapped out as well. We usually don't know some experiences are lessons until we go through them, and sometimes we may not like what we are given. Most of the time, spirit knows best. As you know, I have a mentor who is incredibly knowledgeable and who keeps me sane and grounded. We always have a laugh when I call Rose, and she gives me a slap from spirit: she wants me to see things from another perspective. What I have learnt is that whilst I am learning, so are my children, and it is my job to be the voice of reason to help their growth. This happened when one of my children was going for their car licence. For years, Rose has said that spirit knows best and they are in control of some situations and will help us develop our soul's growth even if the situations are not entirely favourable, it is meant for us to learn a lesson.

How often have you thought you were going to get something, and it didn't happen? You feel deflated, angry, frustrated and at some point, and might say why is this happening to me?

This is what my child went through when they didn't get their licence on their first go. They came home wondering why me? I remember them saying

"Someone up there hates me, because this would've been the best day of my life if I had gotten my licence." Later on, they calmed down and I spoke to them. I said, *"there is always a reason why things happen, and spirit always knows best, you just don't know why yet"*. I was speaking to Rose the same day and told her the story and she commented and said that spirit had saved them, and I didn't know what that meant until the next day.

I received a phone call from my child, and they asked if I would pick them up from work early. Darrin went and picked them up and when they arrived home, I took one look at Darin and my child and I knew something had happened. Darrin told me the story, my child was invited to go to a party the night before, and because they weren't feeling well, they didn't go. They had been seeing someone for a while and quite liked this person. The next day at work they turned on their phone and saw pictures from the party that weren't favourable - they were upset. We spoke about the situation, and I realised why they didn't get their licence. I sat my child down and said:

"Do you realise that spirit saved you the other day when you didn't get your licence?" They looked at me.

"If you would've had your licence and you found out what happened at the party, what would you have done?" I asked. They sat there. I said, 'you would've gone to the party and probably had an argument and it may have gone further, you never know". I also pointed out that their frame of mind would not be where it was supposed to be, and they could have had an accident. Spirit was in control of that and I thanked them for saving my child.

Another example of spirit knowing best, was when my husband Darrin was forced to leave his old job and review his career path. For a month, I was hearing in my head from my Angels:

"Darrin needs to look for another job." I told Darrin how insistent my Angels were, and he agreed with me, but didn't actively look. The voices didn't stop and a month later, he attended a conference overseas, and he came home from work one day early. His boss gave him six weeks to look for a new job. I looked at him stunned, but I could hear my subconscious saying I told you so. Darrin couldn't believe it, but I reminded him that he wanted to look for another job, so spirit had forced his hand. I would usually go into panic mode straight away, but I had an overwhelming feeling that spirit had already sorted things out and they had control of the situation. They told me Darrin would find another job within the six weeks, and he did. Because spirit gave me a heads up about Darrin's job, I learnt to give it to God and leave it in his hands, and that's what I did. When something is out of your control, sometimes you just need to let it go and allow other opportunities to come through. Spirit always knows best, and they will always give us a warning of things to come - even though we don't understand it at the time. When this happens, you need to have faith and go with the flow, because at the end of the day, the lessons we learn in life, are for our highest and best purpose.

15

Gain, Learn, Know & Understand

In 2018, I experienced a massive growth in my soul, both personally and professionally. I was finally learning and putting the pieces of the puzzle together. Over the years, my mentor Rose would give me information and tools to help me learn and she would always say:

"It's nothing unless you apply what you know, and when you do this you will understand what I have been trying to teach you." It's like when you finally understand the maths equation your teacher has been teaching you, the penny had dropped so to speak.

At the beginning of 2018, I had my year mapped out. I had a reading the year before, and spirit said I was going through a transformation and there would be a lot of changes occurring in the year. I was so excited and thought these transformations and changes would be focused on my professional work. I was even promised by a professional advertising agency that they would market me and help me travel to different locations and get my name out there, but these turned out to be only empty promises.

Now I am sitting in my living room in December 2018, and 2019 is just around the corner, and I am reflecting on the year and what I have learnt and how I have grown. I have had a considerable soul growth. We are only here to help our soul grow; we are not here for money, fame and fortune. If you receive this good luck, I would be the first person to congratulate you. Before we were born, we said to God:

"This is what I want to experience, to enhance my individual's soul's growth." The experiences we go through in life, are things we must encounter to help us grow and move forward, because looking or remaining stuck in the past will get us nowhere. Sometimes it's hard to move forward, and some people may feel they are trapped with nowhere to go. In my experience, the only person you can count on to move forward is yourself. It's up to us, because we have come here on earth with individual contracts to complete. One of Rose's mottos is:

"Gain, Learn, Know, Understanding." I didn't understand this motto until this year. As individuals through our experiences, both spiritually and physically, we gain the information needed to help us grow. When the time is right, we learn from our experiences. This could take, minutes months or years: it depends on whether it is the right time. Once we have learnt our lesson, we know where our journey is going, because it feels right, and we can take the next step. The last piece of the puzzle is understanding how all the pieces come together to make a perfect jigsaw. In my experience, this doesn't take five minutes, days or weeks, it might take a lifetime, but in the end if we get to our destination that's all that matters. It is when our soul is ready to complete its agreement with God.

Rose's motto became significant to me this year as a mum and as a professional medium. Being a mum is the most rewarding vocation. I am a mother to three children, Cameron, Elyse and Brooklyn and they all have similar and individual traits. Like everyone, they have come here with their own soul contracts, and their choices and experiences are their own. Rose told me:

"We are all God's children" and when I reflected on her words, I realised how true this was. Our children are on loan to us, just as we are on loan to our parents. It is up to us to fulfil our contracts. As a parent, there have been times when I believed I have known better than my children, because I am older. How often did you roll your eyes when your parents or an older person would say to you:

"I should know, because I am older than you?" This was the case with myself and my children. In some circumstances I did know better and I tried to communicate this to my children. But in some instances, the result of their actions would have consequences I couldn't do anything about.

My lesson as a mum this year was to get out of my own space and my children's. I had one daughter entering her teens, and the other daughter commencing her sixteenth year and a son reaching the end of his teens. Each child was going through their individual lessons at different stages of their lives, and as a parent I had to adapt to these varying levels of maturity. This year with my sixteen-year-old daughter was emotionally challenging. Sixteen is a very challenging age for a young person, and it is a normal age to try and push the barriers with their parents. Being a mother and a medium, the energy between both people can be difficult and explosive. I am not the only medium to experience this and I won't be the last. I hope writing this from my perspective may help another person, even if it is one person at a time.

I am also an empath, and what this means is that I feel and take on other peoples or living things emotions, especially when they are going through a difficult time in their lives. I feel their energy. If a person is going through a break-up and their heart is aching, I feel everything they are feeling. It's the energy around this person that could be dense, overwhelming and it makes it hard to breath. It's fine, though, as I have learnt to deal and live with this. If anyone experiences this or is an empath, the best way to let go of another person's energy is to say:

"If this is not mine, I let it go," and breathe in and out. The most important thing to remember is the intention when it comes to any prayers or letting go. Words are just words when you say them, but if you put intention behind the words and really feel it, that's more effective.

My daughter has been subjected to bullying for most of her school life. This escalated during this school year when she was in year ten. The hardest thing to go through as a parent is to see your child suffer at the hands of another. To feel helpless because you could not be there every second of every day to help them face whatever is happening. I have always said to my kids:

"Bullying is the highest form of compliment," because most of the time the bully is jealous of that person they are bullying. Throughout my life and especially in my junior years of school, I was teased because I was different and because I went through this, it was hard to watch my child go through this as well. I wanted to be the protector and fight for her. But I knew that she had come here to learn her own lessons and complete a part of her jigsaw. I needed to recognise that it was not up to me to be the one to deal with what she was going through. I could only to be a support network and be there when she needed me.

When the bullying started, her moods began to change, and she went from an outgoing young woman to an argumentative, isolated and nasty person at times. This was not a good environment to be in, especially when I am a naturally emotional person. I am a Cancerian and my friend Yoe says Cancerians are sooky, psychic and sensitive. It's the old saying - when your child is hurting so are you. This was the case with me, and I admit I did not handle the situation correctly. When my daughter told me about the bullying, my emotions got the better of me. The questions started: I asked so many why and what happens that I didn't realise my daughter didn't want me to ask questions at all: she wanted me to just listen to her.

Because I was bullied as a child, all my insecurities rose to the surface again, and it felt like I was reliving my youth. This was not what my daughter needed from me. During the past few years, depression and suicide have increased, and I was worried my daughter might fall into deep depression. As suicide amongst all ages has definitely increased, I would initially bring through in a reading one suicide every three months and now it is up to ten a week. A family members best friend had committed suicide earlier in the year, and I had met them once, and they were young and vibrant. They had their whole life ahead of them. So, this was very real for me.

At one point, I became angry with spirit and asked them:

"You tell me everything, I know when things are going to happen to people, places and things, but you did not tell me this was occurring in my daughter's life?" The response from spirit and God was

"You weren't meant to know, this is her life and the lessons are hers, how she deals with them is up to her. It is not your place to interfere with her soul's growth." The message was short and sweet and had a major impact. Of course, God was right, and I took a step back.

There is so much to thank Rose for, and she helped me see things clearer. My daughter Elyse and Rose share the same astrological sign and are very much alike. Rose is my go-to girl when it comes to understanding my daughter. I realised because of my vulnerabilities; I was expecting too much of my daughter. I was told to stop interfering, and let her fight her own battles. Knowing your children and how to handle them is the most important thing, I learnt. Listening to Elyse, and what she wanted from me was the key. I remember saying to Darrin one night that I was a bad parent and I had done a poor job of parenting. I asked my Angels what to do and I heard them say to just be there. In the past, I would react to situations by yelling and getting too involved and this led to arguments. I didn't react the way I normally did this time and I said nothing. Consequently, this spoke volumes. I became a listener and if someone asked for my opinion, I gave it. I experienced periods of hyperventilation, and I knew I had to help myself. A new guide came to me, and her name was Maeve and when I looked up her qualifications: one was the use of oils, just like my two friends, Stacy and Yoe, who were aromatherapists and they were advocating oils to help different ailments. I started to use a blend called liquid Xanax, and it was a life saver. I knew I didn't want or need antidepressants, and I started to use natural blends that worked for me. I have always advocated Spirit and my Angels will always show you the way when the time is right, and this was my time.

Towards the end of the year, my daughter came to me and broke down, and told she was being physically and emotionally bullied by another person. She broke down and cried in my arms and even though I wanted to scream and shout, all I could do was to hold her in my arms and tell her I loved her.

This year, spiritually and professionally, my soul gained knowledge about the true meaning of quality versus quantity. As I previously said those four words - gain, learn know and understand - were significant in applying what I already knew. I spoke about quality versus quantity, and it wasn't until this year that I understood the real meaning behind these four words. I am a professional medium, and I individually read for people every day, but I also perform platform events for my own shows. My shows gathered large enough crowds in previous years, and I am always amazed at how many people want to see me live. My motto has always been:

"The people who need to be there, will be there," and this has been the case. I have been extremely blessed to have sold out shows. But in 2018, we promised our relatives we would travel to the South Coast to do a show. Darrin was hoping to get as many people there as he could. Because I was new to the area and not well-known, we struggled to sell a lot of tickets, the turnout was eighty people and it was exceptional. We had a fabulous night, filled with many memories and experiences. In the next two months, we decided to travel to the Central Coast to do a show in remembrance of a dear friend's love one. I had journeyed there

the year before, and it was a sold-out show. We were hoping this would be the case this time. There were less people there than the South Coast event, and Darrin was wondering why. We could rationalise, that it was the time of year we planned it and people were getting ready for Christmas, or people didn't know the area. But the main reason for this was to teach me the true meaning of quality versus quantity.

I always get nervous before every show, and this was not any different. I knew the people who were meant to be there were there and the Central Coast show had a special place in my heart. The show was amazing, and spirit never missed a beat: they were incredible and the messages they delivered were inspiring. After every night, I always debrief with my mentor Rose. Whilst were discussing this event, she acknowledged my lesson in quality versus quantity. She said that spirit only brought the people that needed to be there at that time, and because I had an intimate group of people, spiritual messages were able to be given to more people. They were able to receive messages and give them as well. I knew spirit and my Angels wouldn't let me down, and God always had a higher plan for me. In both occasions, quality messages were given at the right time and to the people who needed their loved one's support. I understood that it didn't matter how many people came to events and worrying about filling the auditorium doesn't matter. Giving quality readings with a personal touch is the most important thing I can do. God is always in control of what will happen in our lives.

"Spirit will always have it their way, and things will work out for your highest and best purpose," Rose once told me. Now I understand quality verses quality.

16

Knowing the Right Time to Communicate with Spirit

My spiritual journey has had a lot of lessons. Learning which ones to translate is part of my ongoing spiritual growth and in 2015, I started seeing spirits in heaven before they had already passed. This is a journey that has been quite rewarding, gratifying and truly amazing.

As I have already discussed in a previous chapter, spirit taught me that some individual souls do what I like to call a try before you buy before they pass on. This means their soul is preparing for the final journey home. This might take a few weeks, months or even years. You know a person is making their journey home when they start to talk about their loved ones a lot and ask questions about heaven. They are also very sleepy all the time, and if a person has a terminal illness, they will sometimes go into a coma. I have had clients tell me about their experience if they were there when their loved one passed, saying they knew the person was gone, even if their body was still there. I believe our soul leaves our body and crosses over into heaven, and our body takes three days to catch up. People might experience strange things happening in the house, or around them such as knocking on doors, lights turning on and off or being woken up in the middle of the night and sensing someone is standing there. This is our loved ones letting us know they are okay and still around us.

As I was developing the skill of seeing spirit before their body had parted this life, I was concerned that I couldn't give people any proof, and I thought people might think I was making it all up. My validation came when Darrin's grandfather passed away. Poppa had been sick for a while, and his health was deteriorating rapidly. At the time, my youngest daughter was in hospital herself, and one morning a friend of mine called me on my mobile out of the blue and said she had a dream. My friend was visiting Queensland, and she dreamt that she was walking along the beach and a lady walked up to her and smiled and she was with an elderly gentleman. She said her name started with M and that she knew the gentleman walking with her. Darrin's aunty and Popppa's sister had died a few months before, and her name was May. My friend didn't know my daughter was in hospital, or that Poppa was very sick and going to pass.

That same day I left the hospital my daughter was in and came home because I was quite sick and started vomiting. Darrin went back to the hospital to stay with our daughter. But that day became very unusual, because our doorbell kept ringing all the time, and no-one was there. I felt a presence around me. I didn't think it was Poppa. Darrin was quite close to his grandfather, and every time I called Darrin or mentioned his name, the doorbell would ring three times, each time. I felt like I was going nuts. That night, Poppa passed away and I recognised these were his signs to tell me he was crossing over and was fine. In life, he was a practical joker, so it made sense in spirit he was having fun with us as well.

What happened over these three days made sense when I was talking to my mother in law and Poppa's daughter. I explained that I was developing another level of spiritual growth, and I referred to the three-day rule where your soul crosses over, and three days later your body catches up. My mother-in-law Val, said:

"That's funny, because, three days before Poppa died, my doorbell wouldn't stop ringing periodically, and that has never done that before." I knew without a doubt that it was Poppa's way of letting her know he was there and was up to a little mischief as well.

The next instance that convinced me about the three-day rule was during a reading with a lovely young gentleman who told me he was a sceptic, but he was compelled to come and have a reading with me. I received a phone call from this client asking if there was any availability. At the time, I was very booked up. However, I found an opening and I called him to offer it to him. He couldn't make that appointment, and I thought that would be the end of it. A week later, another spot became available and I called him and asked him if he would like the appointment. To our surprise, that day was the only day he had off from his busy schedule. He came for the reading, and as soon as he walked into the room, I could see a gentleman walking in with him and standing behind him.

"Oh, by the way, your father is here, he is standing right next to you," I blurted out.

"My father's not dead." My heart stopped, and I was so apologetic. "But he is very sick and dying of cancer." His father had deteriorated in a week and his son had gone to Sydney to be with him, and that's why he couldn't make the previous appointment the week before.

I started the reading, and my Angels said to me loud and clear that this was where I could put what I was learning into practice. I explained the three-day rule to my client. The man was stunned, because he could recognise all of his dad's qualities that I mentioned during the reading. His dad communicated where his cancer was, what his hospital room looked like, and what he was saying and doing with his son the day before his son came to the reading. His father communicated specific details of what would happen before and after he died, and he was very insistent that I relay the right information. During the reading, the young man's father passed on a lot of information that his son validated, and there were things that his son was confused about because it hadn't happened yet.

A couple of months later, I received a beautiful email from this young man. He wrote that he admitted that he was a little sceptical at the beginning of our session, but he changed his mind within a few minutes. He wrote to me three days after my reading with him to tell me that his father passed away peacefully. Whilst reading the email I was so excited because I was given proof from spirit about what I was learning, and its significance was confirmed when I continued reading the email. The young man said he felt like I had prepared him for his dad's passing, and this meant a great deal to me. I believe that everyone deals with grief differently, and there is no right or wrong way to grieve. It is important to remember people need to grieve in their own way and it is not up to another person to tell someone how to grieve or to move on, everyone is different. Since I communicate with a lot of people who are grieving, I tell them what spirit has taught me about grief. When a loved one passes, the person left behind will never get over it or accept it, but they will learn to live with it. This is what the young man wrote to me in his email, and was very grateful for what I told him. Being in life and living each day is moving forward, but you don't have to do leaps and bounds: just do it one step at a time. Our loved ones are standing in front of us, encouraging us not to sit down and wallow in self-pity. We need to be able to live whilst missing them. Spirit has taught me that when you are in constant self-pity and not being productive, meeting up with them would be difficult. I am not saying you won't meet up with your family in spirit, because you will. But you will make it difficult for yourself if you don't live in life because that's why we are here. It was a privilege to read for this young man and bringing the information through from his dad was a blessing. Knowing I gave comfort to someone during a period of great sorrow was truly amazing. The email ended with him thanking me for the work that I do and gave reassurance to people that our loved ones are happy and at peace in spirit is comforting, I always have the same reply:

"*All thanks to spirit because I am just the voice.*"

Knowing the right time to communicate with spirit is important and, in my experience, you cannot force a loved one to talk to you just because you are ready. There are many reasons why they might not come through. If a person has been unwell for a long time, when they cross over into heaven, they may need to visit the healing room. This is about healing their soul and enhancing their vibration. This is equally important for a person who died tragically. If you think about it, when you are sick our energy is dull or unresponsive compared to our usual vibrant self, therefore, to restore these vibrations, we need some healing which is done in the healing room. Another reason why they might not come through in a reading may be because the family isn't ready. This does not mean they won't come through ever, there might be something standing in their way such as grief. One thing I do know about spirit is that they do not like to be told what they are to do so they will not jump through hoops just because you have asked them to do it. I work on the idea that if a person was not overly enthusiastic in life, they may not be overly enthusiastic in spirit. However, I have had on some occasions during a reading had a loved one that was expressive and very communicative, but in life was very quiet. I remember my son's eighteenth birthday, his friend who is very quiet and reserved, had a couple of drinks and you could not shut him up. I had a whole conversation with him, and I have known him all his life. What spirit has taught me anything can happen in a reading and it is awesome when it does.

I have had many people contact me after their loved one has passed away, and they want a reading straight away. In my experience, just because you are ready for them to communicate with you doesn't mean it is the right time. You need to ask yourself, why do you want to talk to them? Is it because you want to know they are all right? Did you not get to say goodbye, are there unresolved issues? Or are you feeling guilty? These questions are relevant, and I can sympathise with my clients. Despite this, spirit will always come through when it is the right time. This is equally important when a family member wants to communicate with their family in heaven. I have had people calling to ask me to fit their spouse in for a reading because their loved one has passed recently. The spouse's behaviour isn't what is used to be, and they believe having a reading would help their spouse, and they would feel better and things would be back to where it is supposed to be. Like spirit, I believe you cannot force your spouse to have a reading even though your intentions come from the heart. It may be too soon, and the grieving process is very different for everyone. When the spouse is ready to have a reading, spirit will make it happen at the right time. Something to think about! If you ever find yourself in this position, say to yourself:

"Why do I want my love one to have this experience?"

"What are my intentions?" You might come for a reading to communicate with your loved one, but remember you need to consider your spouse. Do they want to have a reading or are you trying to control the emotional situation?

I did a group reading session for a friend of mine and her family early in 2016, and in that reading, an uncle came through and spoke about their father. He was particularly insistent about his leg. He said that his brother had to look after his leg and to watch out for a clot forming in his right leg. The whole family knew about their father's leg, but they said this had already happened and that he had already gone into hospital for this. I said okay and thought this was then end of it. However, their uncle was insistent, and kept bringing this clot in the right leg up.

In December of that year my friend contacted me to say that her father was very sick and a month later, he passed away from a clot in his right leg, there were other factors that contributed to his illness, but this was the main cause of death. Soon after the funeral, I started to receive messages from family members asking to book an appointment to see me as soon as possible. I was happy to book them in when I had an appointment, but I had a feeling their father may take a while to come through because he might be attending the healing room. A month after he had passed, he was communicating with me, I would be getting ready for work or to go out and I would hear "I am ready", and I knew exactly who it was.

"Well when do you want your family to come because I am fully booked for some time?" I replied.

"When the time is right, you will know?" He replied. I thought *well, that's a bit cryptic*. One thing I do know about spirit is that they will make it happen when it's supposed to happen, and that is why I do not have a cancellation list. My friend's father was right. In March, my family and I booked to go on a cruise, and my friend was also on the cruise. I found out that her dad had booked the cruise as well and was going to come with his wife before he got sick. As soon as I sat down to talk to my friend and her mother, her father was in my ear saying he was there, and he was ready to talk to them. I politely told him that I was on holidays, and would he please wait until I was back at work and I could speak with him. I knew as soon as I was back, there would be a vacancy and his family members could come and communicate with him. I read for his granddaughter on the Monday night after she attended her uncle's wedding. I now knew why he was so insistent, and he wanted his son to know he was at the wedding.

What I have learnt from spirit is that being ready to communicate with their loved ones also depends on how evolved their soul is. If they are an old soul, and they have done this before, they would communicate and come through in a reading quickly. I have had a person come through within twelve hours of crossing over. If you are a new soul which translates that you have not had many past lives, the transition of communicating with their loved ones may take a little while, in both cases spirit will know when it is the right time to communicate.

17

Inspirational Story

When I was young, my mum would tell me I could be anything I wanted to be. At that time my first passion was performing in ballet. I was a shy child, and I was going through things in my life and I wanted to escape, and dancing became my outlet. It was the strong arm to hold me, or a place to call home and be accepted without any judgements. I loved it more than anything and it became my happy place.

I continued to dance throughout my childhood and adolescent years, and through hard work and commitment, I became quite a good dancer. Professionals even asked me to make it my career. Instead, I chose another path in life, and this meant going to University and giving up my dream. Of course, I have missed dancing and over the years I have thought of what might have been, but my first passion lives on in my daughters, and seeing the enjoyment they have with their dancing means the world to me.

I grew up, finished my university course, started to work full time, met my husband and I had three beautiful children. It wasn't until I was in my early thirties that my true passion emerged - being the voice of spirit. At the time, I didn't know I had embarked on an incredible journey. At first, it started because I wanted to leave my current job, and I had to earn an income. I didn't know what else to do. I knew I wanted to stay home and look after my children. I wanted to do something that would allow me to stay at home and it would be a bonus if I loved what I did. I remember thinking how much I loved my Angels, and knew I wanted to work with them, so I looked to them for guidance and what an incredible journey it has been.

My son was finishing his High School Certificate in 2017 and I remembered what my mum had said to me:

"You can be anything you want to be." As I was sitting outside, thinking about where I have come from, I have to say a massive thank you to my Angels for their love and support. I have been incredibly lucky to meet beautiful people and working with spirit is an absolute privilege.

It makes me think of mum's words all the time, and I definitely can do anything. Yes, there will be good and bad moments in life, but, the good will always outweigh the bad.

I have been told my purpose in life is to give peace to people, and to do this is an absolute joy and privilege. Sometimes I sit in my bedroom reflecting on my journey as a medium and my experiences. No money or wealth could replace the memories I have, and I give thanks to everyone I have met and will meet on this journey. I also give thanks to spirit and my Angels for their unfailing support.

Faith has had so much meaning in my life from the past to the present, but whatever I am going through I know that faith will be my friend and I can rise to any challenge.

I am sure, like many writers, before they start writing their book, they have to find some inspiration. My inspiration comes from many things: from the people I have met, my family, my mentor, my friends and other likeminded people. I always have been inspired by my Angels and spirit. There are so many ways to be inspired, it could be watching YouTube or watching a young girl singing on X Factor, and going through to the live shows. It could be going to spiritual church and seeing a medium's demonstration and being inspired by their words. Inspiration could come from walking down the street and seeing someone being kind to another. Actions always speak volumes.

The inspiration for this chapter came from two places: one was watching a video on Facebook and being inspired by the young fourteen-year-old who I mentioned above. The second came from an email I was sent. I conducted a group reading for six beautiful people the Friday night before I received the email, and in the reading, I spoke about someone going to America on a cruise. At the time, no-one understood the information, but I passed it on. A couple of days later, I received an email from a beautiful lady called Lisa. She told me after leaving, she and her family were unsure who was going on the trip to the USA. A couple of days later, when a nurse had come to one of her family's member's house for treatment, they mentioned that they had to rebook a certain date for the patient's treatment because they were taking their family on a cruise to the USA. After reading this, I had an overwhelming urge to write about inspiration. I knew then it was my Angels asking me to write.

Once I had finished part of my chapter, I put it on my Facebook page - Angels Amongst Us and asked for honest opinions and I was blown away with the comments. Inspiration was a frequent comment. I remember meeting a young girl and she said after our meeting that she had read my first book and how much of an inspiration I was. I have never thought of myself as an inspiration, it is who I am. I have always thought that people who inspire others are the ones that have survived difficult times. Inspiration can come in the smallest of ways: a hello, respect, fulfilling a dream or survival. I realised when someone is inspired, their whole being starts to tingle, and most of us will get goose bumps. When you see something that inspires you, it shouldn't end there, it is up to the individual to use that inspiration and make some changes in their lives and be an inspiration to someone else.

My friend Stacy summed up inspiration in a comment she left me on my Facebook page:

"It is with your heart, your soul, your strength and your raw courage that you are able to fulfil your dreams, and live out your passions, with this you are able to give hope, inspire, ignite, fuel, heal, help guide and drive others and this not only makes you a beautiful person but a role model. It truly makes you an Earth Angel."

There are many ways people are inspired. One way can be social media. Used correctly, social media can be a great way to get an individuals message across. I have never been a huge fan, because I have seen the damage it can cause. But I have also experienced the positives of social media as well. My next story is an example of how I was inspired by a young man and the work he does every day. One night, I had an urge to look through Facebook, and I saw a live video of a man talking about the work he does. I am not a person who goes onto Facebook every chance I get, unlike my husband, but something told me to listen to this man's story and I did.

He was doing a live feed, telling his story of how he got into the business of helping children who were dying of terminal illnesses. He explained that he travels all around the country talking to children in hospitals and schools. He even dresses up as a superhero. He explained how he got started. His grandmother came to him in a dream and told him he would be going out into the world and talking to children to be there when they crossed over. As I was listening to the video, I realised I could relate to everything he was saying. My own grandmother came to me in a vision and told me I would be doing the work I am doing. He spoke about how it was a privilege to sit and hold hands with a child when they took their last breath to let them know that they weren't alone. He said that God had given this gift to him for a reason, because he knew he would be the one that could do the work. I admire all medical staff who are faced with death every day and their loving energy and care are to be commended. This includes parents and love ones of terminal ill individuals, especially children.

The young man talked about the concerns human beings may have in life are meaningless, because when you sit and evaluate your life and put into perspective what you are going through compared to a child or individual facing a terminal illness, it doesn't come close. Why did he choose to be with these children when they crossed over? It would be a hard thing to do, but he said that God gave him this gift of taking away a child's pain, and that is his purpose in life. I have the privilege to see the child when they are healthy and happy in spirit. I have recently said that my speciality is bringing through children that have crossed over. It was something I kept to myself. Another medium told me this was my speciality before I became a professional medium.

I learnt that everyone has purpose in life, even if we don't know what it is at the time. God will always show us the way when it is time. I believe people cross our paths at certain times in our lives, and they are there to teach us another way of doing things and hopefully inspire us to change our lives or show us we are on the right track. I was so grateful to my friend for sharing this video, because it validated that my career choice was a gift. There are people in life I call earth Angels, and this young man is one of them. I realised that my work is equally important because whilst this man is in the physical world to give comfort and love to the child before they cross over, my job is to validate that love is eternal and that our souls never die.

Spiritual Fingerprints

Everyone is unique.
They have their own set of characteristics,
Their own growth,
Lessons,
What does a spiritual fingerprint do?

In 2017 I was at the point in my life where I was analysing why my life's journey happened the way it did. I knew I had always had it from an early age. To find my path, I had to experience other professions. Dancing at an early age taught me about confidence, my body, being part of a group and discipline. Nursing taught me about human nature, human anatomy, disease processes and being part of a select community who helps to preserve human lives. Even though being a mother and wife isn't regarded as a profession it has taught me about loving another human being unconditionally, patience, strength, organisational skills, belonging to someone, partnerships, and most of all finding out essentially, who am I.

In my experience, people have often commented that they want to be like me or communicate with spirit the way I do. I have often heard people say that they believe this person is better than this person. I have always had the belief that we are no better than anyone else because we are all unique. Our characteristics are exclusive to us and no one can be like another person. People will try to adapt to be like other people but will miss what makes that person distinctive. It's like baking your grandmother's cake: The ingredients are there, but there is something missing and it is usually the special touch of how grandma made the cake. That's the uniqueness of an individual the special qualities of that person.

When someone says they think another person is better, I believe it is usually that they may resonate with that person's ability or personality. Not everyone is going to get on with everyone; there are people I do not resonate with or understand, and I am sure there have been people that haven't resonated with me. It is important to recognise that everyone is different, and this is what makes the world what it is.

Recently, I was invited to do a platform event for a charity alongside two other well-respected and talented mediums. It was a great night. I like to watch other mediums work. It is always interesting to see how they bring spirit through. The next day, I was sitting in my bedroom thinking about the day and I realised why spirit gave me an opportunity to learn. Rose would say it doesn't matter how the information comes from spirit, as long, as it does, and this is exactly what I saw. All three of us had different ways to bring spirit through for their loved ones, and everyone who received the information understood. It truly doesn't matter how we communicate with spirit, as long as we come from the right space. I believe no-one is better than anyone else, but they might be more experienced and have their own unique qualities. This is refreshing to see, and you never know you may learn something like I did.

18

Blueprints

It blows my mind there are billions of people in the world and no two individuals are the same: everyone has unique fingerprints and personalities. Like a fingerprint, spirit has what I like to call a spiritual blueprint unique to them. It is how I distinguish one spirit from another. Because of the work I do, I see a lot of people in the spirit world and in the physical. I strive to bring through my clients' loved ones, and to do this, I ask spirit about characteristics they had in the physical world to prove they are the person to whom the client wants to speak too.

It could be their hair colour or style, their eyes or any distinguishable features that the client would know. I was in a reading once, and a spirit came through, and showed me two different coloured eyes. I thought my mind was playing tricks, but I believe in giving people what I get, and I mentioned to my client that I could see a relative with one blue eye and one green eye. I expected my client to not understand what I was saying but to my surprise, they said:

"Yes, that's my dad he had two different coloured eyes!"

People will have distinctive traits in the physical and the spirit world. We are only here on this earth to grow and evolve as souls and this means learning lessons that are assigned to us before we are born. I believe we have a blueprint, and before we are born, we say to God or whoever you believe in: we are going to experience different lessons and by learning these lessons we are enabling our soul's growth. Some people might call it karma, but I believe in lessons that help to evolve our souls. There is no right or wrong way to learn.

Spirit also has lessons when they reach heaven. If you have not completed your tasks here on earth before you cross over, you will be expected to take steps towards completing them in heaven. I like to mention this to clients whose loved ones have committed suicide. What someone believes about suicide is their belief - it is not up to me to change their mind. However, I have read for many spirits who have taken their own lives, and in my experience, they will always come through and talk to their family or friends and say that God has given them a choice: to be born again and learn the lessons they should've learnt, or to stay in heaven and be assigned to help people not to take the same road they did. This person would be given a sign, and signs can be seen so many ways. If spirit wants you to know something, they will make it happen. It could be during a conversation someone is having, or a person is compelled to watch a documentary or read a book that may help them.

By helping people work towards completing their lessons in the physical world, the spirit is also completing their lessons they didn't before they crossed over. In my experience spirit will be placed in a similar situation the physical person is going through and by helping each other the lessons are being accomplished. However, we can get help from spirit, but it is up to the individual to notice the signs and want to better themselves. What I have encountered is that spirit is always patient and will wait until the individual is ready.

19

How Do Our Loved Ones Know Our Vibration and When to Come to Us?

One Sunday morning, I was lying in bed. Out of the blue, I had a message from spirit.

"You must create a subscription page for your Facebook page - Angels Amongst Us." I thought this would be great, because it would get my face out there and when I start to spread my wings people would see who I am through live feeds. For many years, I had received private messages asking me about spirit, and their experiences. I knew what it was like to ask about experiences, and I didn't know who to ask. Until I met my teachers and Rose, I felt a little lost and confused. My mission was to create a page that supported people, where I was able to do live feeds and answer the questions people had. After I explained to Darrin what spirit's message was, he quickly sought out a programme to help with the subscription, and it was up and running in no time. It quickly became a place where people could go to write about their experiences and share their stories. There were beautiful personal stories, and the support imparted by the group was amazing. I quickly realised that what I originally thought was my mission was not what spirit had in mind, and that was okay. Darrin didn't create a page that was meant to get me out there: I was the catalyst. I was meant to create an environment where people felt safe to write their personal stories and not be ridiculed or to ask questions they would normally avoid because of trolls, ultimately it was to bring people together. I was asked a question one night during a live feed:

"How do we know when we are in spirit or know where to go to speak to our loved ones that are still in the physical?" At first, I didn't think I could answer the question, and I said as much. But then spirit took over and explained it perfectly. Everyone has a fingerprint or a blueprint that is unique to them, so your soul and essence is unique to you as a physical being and a spiritual person. Your vibration is unique to you. Your loved ones would have already connected with you through love, physical touch, thoughts, communication, and personal experiences before they crossed over. The vibrations would have blended together. When our loved ones go to heaven, our memories of them would create a unique vibration. Our loved ones connect with your vibration. Like a memory card, it stores information and when we need this information, we can retrieve it. The most important connection we have with our loved ones in spirit is love.

I believe our life experiences become fingerprints that are stored in our aura and enteric field. When it is time to understand them, we can call upon them as needed. They are stored and never lost. This was the case when I was writing this book. Spirit would give me valuable information that resonated with me during a reading, and when I was finished, I didn't remember. I would sit and try to remember the information but was unable to until I had to use it.

"What are you doing?" I asked Rose once. She wasn't looking at me but staring into the distance.

"I'm working." I didn't understand what that meant until I asked for an explanation. It meant that sometimes, we can be in the physical, but our spirit is somewhere else. When someone has a faraway look in their eyes, their spirit is talking to the universe or other spirits. This happened that same night. There was a group of us, and Rose discussed memory recall - déjà vu. Rose was explaining astral travel, which means your physical body stays in a stationary position and your spirit leaves your body and travels through the astral plane to various places or visits with spirit. I have visited people in a different house I have never met before. Astral travel mainly occurs when someone is asleep, but it can happen during awake periods.

Regarding déjà vu, our spirit may have left our body, and astral travelled somewhere we want to go or need to be. I believe there are no coincidences: if we are meant to be at a place at a certain time the universe will make it happen when the time is right. Therefore, when we travel to a certain destination, we immediately feel familiar with the surroundings, because we have been there in spirit and the pieces of the puzzle start to come together. As a result, the imprint that was stored when we astral travelled will appear, and you will understand why you were put there for your soul's development.

If you think about it, if we think of déjà vu as a past life incident, then buildings that are here now won't be in the past, so how do you remember the buildings from a past life?

20

Having Faith in Yourself and in Spirit

When I was writing my first book, my husband was made redundant. I wrote about coping with something that was out of my control and being a control freak, because I wanted to know about something that wasn't about me but affected me. As I was writing this book, I was again faced with Darrin's changing career. Again, Darrin was forced to review his life and evaluate what he desired in a career.

In early May 2017, I knew Darrin wasn't happy in his current job. He wasn't sleeping well, he looked tired all the time and his moods would change often. One day I was washing up, and spirit said Darrin needed to start looking for another job. I passed on the information. At the time, Darrin was getting ready to go overseas on a business trip for work. Spirit was persistent, and I told Darrin again. He took my message semi-seriously and said he would start looking for a new job seriously when he returned. I knew that would be too long to wait, but Darrin said he wanted to be loyal to the company because they had paid for his trip, and he didn't want to burn bridges if he got a new job. I agreed with Darrin, but I couldn't shake the uneasy feeling I was getting about what spirit said in the first place. I just had to respect Darrin's wishes and see what happened.

Three days after he returned from the trip, Darrin was called into the office, and he was told he needed to find another job. I knew something was wrong when he came home that day. He told me what had happened.

"I told you, what spirit had said to do."

"I was going to start looking this week," Darrin tried to defend himself. I knew this probably was true, but I also knew he wouldn't look seriously. He would make excuses not to look. The Angels knew this, so they sped things up a little. I was unusually calm, and this was out of the ordinary for me. I remember standing at the breakfast bar making myself a cup of coffee.

"Why has this happened again? Please, God find him another job?" The reply I received was not what I expected. I heard loud and clear:

"It's sorted." I was a little confused at first.

"Sorry, can you explain please?"

"It's sorted." I crinkled my face.

"Well, what the heck does that mean?" My lesson from God was to have faith in him and to give up trying to control situations I had no control over. Only recently, I was talking to my friend, Emma. She said:

"Every year my faith is tested, and it is around the same time of year." I thought of that, and recognised she was right. Faith has been a big part of my learning as a physical and spiritual soul.

"Maybe I should be an advocate for faith, as mine is tested often." My faith was tested by spirit once again, and I was forced to recall what the true meaning of faith was. Faith is believing in something we can't see, and trusting that when the time is right, God will have a plan and show us in the right time.

Everything happens for a reason, and when one door closes, another door opens to a bigger and brighter future. This was the case with Darrin, even though he was forced to review his career path which was a bit of a blow to him. He was offered a new job, and it was better for him.

21

Seeing Through the Eyes of Our Loved Ones

Accept what is,
Let go of what was,
Have faith in what will be......

At the beginning of every year, I always look back on the preceding year to see if I have learnt my lessons for that year. I always ask what lessons I need to learn in the new year.

One of my lessons for 2019 was to find the magic and passion in my career again. Everyone gets caught up in their schedules. Life can be overwhelming at times and due to time restrictions, we get bombarded with the demands of life. Many people concentrate on what other people were achieving that we ignore our goals. I realised I was doing this in 2018, and I had been trying to control a lot in my life and the lives of my family. I lost sight of what was or wasn't important. I was so caught up in trying to control my children's lives and trying to be a good mother, that I didn't take time to sit down and reflect on the past and acknowledge that I have been a good mum. I nourished them and supported them and created stability. But what I didn't understand, that it was time to let go of them. I have found it quite difficult to see my children maturing and not needing me as much. Sometimes it can feel quite empty, but my logical side says it is time for the chicks to leave the nests, but my emotional side will always know they are a part of me.

Finding the passion in life and my career was important to me. I wanted things done my way, and this included my work. I was becoming too rigid and trying to control things that were out of my control. Many times, my family in spirit had said to relax and have fun. When I did this, the things I worried about were not as important and they worked out the way they were supposed to. I was allowing myself to worry about things that didn't have a major impact in my life. To help myself, I say sorry to myself, my children and spirit for trying to be a control freak. It is challenging to say sorry, and it is equally challenging to admit when you are wrong. But admitting it to yourself first is important for your soul and your true self. When we are rigid, we become selfish and we want things to be done now. As a result, we limit ourselves. But sometimes we don't even know we were rigid or controlling until we are shown by someone else, and then we need to apologise to ourselves.

Finding the magic meant being able to stand alone and walk my talk, because no one could do it for me. I had to complete my lessons for my soul's development. I have my own contract from God, and it is up to me to complete it. I had to stand up and be counted and not worry about what others thought of me. I realised I was expecting too much of myself, and I expected too much of spirit. I had to accept I was trying to be a control freak in my sessions. I fell into the trap of trying to give the client what they wanted and how they expected the session would go rather than leaving it to spirit. I disregarded the first rule of communication with spirit, they are always in control and you give the client what you get and don't try to analyse the reading or information - it is all spirit, not me.

At the start of 2019, the word expectation was clear in my mind. I heard it over and over. After sitting down and listening to my spirit, I figured it out. I admitted to myself that I was taking myself for granted and other people were too. I decided that this year would be my year, and my friendship, companionship or professionalism would be earned. I decided it had to be a two-way path. If someone wasn't respecting me and giving not only receiving, I would let that person go. It could even be little things, like thanking me for a text that I'd sent. I didn't need or want people in my life who only took my energy and time.

At the end of December 2018, my good friend Bobbie, had lost her mother to cancer. One day I was thinking of her, and I fell asleep. I woke to a missed call from her. I went to call her back, but I had an overwhelming feeling to go back to sleep, and I did. I had a very vivid dream from spirit, and it involved her mother, Bobbie and her extended family.

The dream commenced with Bobbie visiting me after her mother's death. We were sitting in my lounge room, and as Bobbie was talking, I noticed her mother standing outside with a lovely smile on her face, looking in the window. Bobbie said she had to go home to arrange the funeral. She walked out the door and her mother stood there, looking through the window again. I walked inside and saw a woman with her husband playing with a little baby boy. On the other side of the room, I saw a lady with her husband sitting playing with a little girl and her brother. I felt the love from Bobbie's mother to these people whom I didn't recognise. Then, I was in hospital looking through the eyes of someone crossing over, and I saw Bobbie bending forward looking into my eyes, placing her hand on my chest and saying goodbye. My eyes closed, and I knew I was gone. I woke up, and called my friend straight away and gave her a summary of the dream. She was so appreciative and said the two families I saw in the dream were her nieces and their families, and Bobbie's goodbye to her mum was how it happened in my dream. I told Bobbie her mother was happy and wanted her to know she was safe, and the memory of what transpired before her death will live forever. On the Saturday of that week, I was reading for a group of people at a high tea, and the same thing happened. I was talking to a lady, and her father came through and showed me his last memory before he crossed over. It was of his wife bending forward and looking into his eyes and she placed her forehead on his and said goodbye as he passed. The daughter was so emotional and grateful as this was what had happened.

I was so amazed with what I saw, and I thought I was developing another level of spiritual awareness. I visited Rose to tell her about my new discovery. I felt so wonderful and privileged for spirit to give me this gift.

"You have always been able to do this, but for some reason you forgot you could do this." I was stunned and she proceeded to do a card reading. The card that represented spiritual lesson was turned over:

"My death was painless". The penny dropped. I now understood spirit's message. It was also about expectations. Because I was so focused on giving my clients what they expected, I overlooked what spirit wanted to say. I wasn't letting the information flow. It was spirit's subtle reminder that people who came to see me experienced moments and knew about the afterlife, because spirit was communicating through me. But they didn't know the in between: the dying and what their loved one was experiencing. By not acknowledging this, I disregarded an important part of death. The in between is the link that sets people free. It sets the person that was suffering free and it sets the people left behind free. They are not suffering anymore, and this helps the people left behind to move forward, knowing their loved ones are happy. I thought of the phrase the circle of life - our life is a circle: the beginning of life is birth; the middle is our death and the ending is going home again. We never die, like a circle - there is no beginning and no end: just a continuous journey.

"You already know death is peaceful, but what does it physically feel like?" I couldn't describe it, only the feeling. She explained the physical encounter as:

"Having aesthetic and drifting off to sleep." Rose had experienced this - a blissful peace.

We all have an analytical mind. I believe this is the part of the brain that tries to process information for us. Expectations sometimes override thoughts. When we want to please another person or we don't want to be wrong, we put pressure on ourselves, making us believe unimportant things are important. This was my lesson, and I thank spirit for showing me the importance of crossing over.

22

Random Messages

How often do you have random thoughts? Or, have you had someone come up to you and say or ask you something random? In the age of Facebook, Instagram, Snapchat and other social websites, I constantly receive random messages on my newsfeed, and sometimes these messages are quotes of the day. They reflect what I have been experiencing or thinking, and their effect on me is astonishing. I love to go onto Facebook and Instagram and post positive quotes that have made it to my page. I believe everyone needs to be uplifted, feel joy or just to make their day with a positive affirmation.

As I have previously mentioned, 2018 was a year of reflection and getting rid of expectations. At the start of 2019, my messages from spirit had changed or more importantly I realised spirits communication with their loved ones were random messages. These messages were not as important, but it was my lesson about expectations, and trying to control the reading. It is always in spirits hands.

At the start of every reading, I talk to my client and outline how I communicate with spirit, as everyone has different ways in connecting with them. The result is always the same - the connection to spirit. The way I interpret the information may differ from other mediums. In my outline, I talk about how I connect to spirit, and I mention how the messages are random and sometimes not what we expect. In my experience, the messages from spirit are not always like the messages we see mediums giving on television. It is not to say that these mediums aren't talented, and the information isn't correct. But the show would be edited, and random messages are not what the public would be interested in. Television is for entertainment. If random information was all that was given, they wouldn't get any ratings. Always remember, what is random to us is not random to spirit. Their messengers are important to them and the way they bring them through is equally important.

The Cambridge English dictionary defines random as: *the definition of random is made, done or happening without a conscious decision.*

There is no method or structure to spirits communication. I give what I get, and this is important when you are a medium. You are spirit's messenger and voice, and your beliefs or judgements cannot influence a reading. You cannot make up the information, because it is unethical, disrespectful and spirit will teach you a lesson that you will not appreciate. So, if the information seems random to people or yourself, it won't be to spirit. Readings aren't always bells and whistles and the surprising scenarios. The information given is what the person needs to know, not what they want to hear. Understanding random messages helped me to understand spirit's voice, and to help me realise that my expectations for how a reading will go will not be obvious.

I always laugh when I meet up with my friend Rodney and we talk about his nan and the messages she wants him to hear. His reaction is always the same whether I'm giving him a reading or telling him about an experience. His reply is random, or that's random.

I first met Rodney early in my career when he along with his partner, Craig came for a reading. From the time we met until now, we all have become lifelong friends. The minute Rodney walked into my reading room; I knew he was there out of curiosity. Many years later, he had told me he didn't believe in the work I do until I brought his beloved grandmother through and she said she was in the room with us. He is the first person to introduce me to the idea of random messages. When I was writing my book, I called him and asked Rodney to tell me about some random experiences he had during our reading. He loves to tell of a few experiences, and they both were in our first session together. Rodney sat down in my room, and immediately I saw an older lady standing next to him and she said the letter J - Rodney confirmed it was his nanna Joan whom he was quite close to. She immediately started talking about bed sheets hanging on the line.

"Why do you hang your washing out at night?'" He just stared at me.

"Yes, I always do my washing at night. I've just hung new bed sheets on the line. "His nan continued to confirm her presence by asking:

"How was your pizza before you came tonight, because you and Craig had it and remember the time, I burnt the pizza?" Rodney just laughed and said Craig and himself did have pizza before they came for their reading, but the funny episode with the burnt pizza. His nan didn't burn the pizza, but when she put the pizza in the oven, she put it on the tray upside down and it didn't cook well.

Rodney loves to tell how I heard him say something in his mind when I bent down during the reading to take a drink. I had to take a break during the session and as I reached down to drink my Mother energy drink, I heard in my head Rodney say:

"That Mother energy drink is very bad for you, why are you drinking that?" After I finished my drink, I turned to him and looked him in the eye.

"Yes, yes Rodney, I know the energy drink is bad for me." Rodney's face turned white and I could see the expression on his face was one of disbelief and thinking that was random.

In my experience, spirits care about the big and little things in our lives. Once I said to a client, that she was eating an ice cream the night before with her daughter. When I delivered the information from her dad, my client just stared at me.

"Yes, that's random." I explained that even though it may not have been important to her, it was important to her father and confirmed that her father was in the room and watching her having fun and quality time with her daughter.

I started a reading one night, and my client's son who died in a car accident came through to his two sisters and his mother. During the reading, he mentioned a wedding that was coming up. His sister started to cry because she was shopping that day with her family for her wedding dress. Her brother mentioned a restaurant in the city they went too, and someone had steak for lunch. This same girl was speechless, because they were shopping in the city and had gone to a restaurant. Her fiancé had a steak for lunch that day. It was a random message to give her, but her brother was so excited that she was getting married. He wanted to let her know he was with the family when they were shopping for a wedding dress and sitting in the restaurant watching her fiancé eat a steak for lunch. The brother was spending quality time with the family.

Recently I took some time out and enjoyed a family holiday cruising the South Pacific. Darrin and I went for a walk on the promenade deck and I noticed everywhere I went people were staring at me. This is not an uncommon occurrence, as this happens quite a lot. The thing is, I don't know any of these people, and I often worry that there is something on my face or that my hair looks funny. On this day, I turned to Darrin and asked him, and he said I looked fine. I let it go, but I knew there was something about this day I needed to know.

Let me explain what it looks like when you meet or see someone who has spirit around them. Have you ever looked at another person and you can not look away? They may look a little brighter, their energy is welcoming, and you feel warm and fuzzy inside. This an example of a person who has spirit around them. On many occasions, when I have met children and babies for the first time, they just smile and look over my shoulder at something we cannot see or they just look at me with a funny expression and I know, they know, I can see and speak to loved ones in heaven. A friend's daughter did exactly this when I first met her, she smiled at me and then looked over my shoulder and talked to someone who wasn't in the physical. Another friend described it perfectly, they said, they would see sparkles around an individual and that they would have a little spark to their step.

I went back to my room on the cruise and I was cleaning up when my stateroom assistant walked in and we began to talk. I told him I was writing a book, and he asked about my profession. I said I was a medium, unsure if he would understand that, I explained I communicate with loved ones who have passed, and I gave an example: a father that may have passed. I knew someone was there next to me, but I didn't know at the time it was this attendant's father. He said his father had passed away a year ago. I looked at him.

"I know, he loves you very much." His dad told me he smoked, and he died of a heart attack. I asked his son about this, and the attendant said yes. He was amazed that his dad came through, and I was honoured to give him the message. The attendant and I continued to talk, and his father said to tell his son that it was okay that he wasn't there when he died. I carefully relayed the message as best I could, so I wouldn't scare his son. When I finished, his son stopped what he was doing, and stared at me. He said his dad was alone in the house when he suffered a massive heart attack. His father knew his son was consumed by guilt because he was working at the time, and I explained this. It was his father's choice to pass away that day, it happened the way he wanted it. Not to say a final goodbye, but farewell until we meet again. The attendant broke down and cried. I knew then why people were staring at me. It wasn't because I have gorgeous curly hair or I look funny, it was because I had a spirit around me.

Maybe these people didn't realise why they were staring, but it highlights that when spirit is around it will give me a heads up when a random moment will happen. I am privileged to give a message to their family. Life is made up of moments, and it is up to us to be in that moment and take every opportunity. You never know when spirit will put you into the path of a random person, and a connection is made that is priceless. There are no coincidences, only random experiences that are given to us to develop and move forward in our lives. Every experience shapes our lives, whether we consider it to be good or bad. It's the getting through the situation that is the important aspect.

I was scrolling through my business page on Facebook one day, and I noticed I had a new review. I am very thankful that people take the time to write about their experiences during a reading - whether it is positive or negative feedback. This day I was drawn to my rating scale, and I had noticed it had dropped slightly. I was curious about what had happened, because it had been steady for so long. I went onto my messages and found negative feedback. I was a little disappointed. Not because of the negative rating, but because I was sad that the person didn't feel I gave them accurate information or what they were hoping for. The message wasn't written in a derogatory manner: they were quite nice to me, but they said because of the reading, they had lost hope in an afterlife. I love what I do, and I truly believe there is life after life and I trust in my Angels, Guides and spirit to give me the correct information, even though we may not understand what they are communicating.

After I finished reading the review, I felt deflated and questioned whether to continue this path. I asked my Angels and God to show me a sign. I opened up Facebook again, and a random Angel message feed came up[from Spiritual & Angel Euphoria - the same day. It said:

"*The Angels are saying to you today...Rise above it, you're better than that! No longer do you have to prove your worth, your worth is already known and admired. You may not know this yet, but the truth of who you are is known to so many, your precious light works in tandem with us. Please keep shinning, you are so precious to us. You've got this.*"

I thanked the Angels for their message of love. I had been seeing a lot of feathers around me, especially in my reading room. Every time I see feathers, I know something will happen after a struggle with faith. This is spirit's way of showing their love and support and to let me know they are with me. The next day was Mother's Day and I went shopping. As I was walking out of the check-out, a lady was waiting for me. She asked me if my name was Judy and when I replied yes, she said:

"I wanted to come and say thank you for all that you do." She went on to tell me she attended one of my events a year ago, and during this event I picked her out of a crowd and the message her loved ones gave her was very comforting. She was going through a hard time, and at the time she was asking her loved ones for help and they replied, "everything will be okay" and it was.

I just hugged her and replied how grateful I was for the feedback as it came at a time when I needed it the most. I knew spirit and my Angels put this beautiful person on my path to let me know that I had to rise above things and keep going. I was so thankful to spirit for orchestrating a random situation which proved to be benefitable to two people who needed comfort and support.

What I had learnt from this experience is that life is not going to be perfect. There will be twists and turns, and you will receive negative feedback and that's okay because everyone is entitled to their opinion.

"No-one gets 100% in their ATAR, so why should life be any different?" Darrin said to me once. When you are dealt a blow, do you react in a negative way and do things that make you feel even worse? Or do you take these knockbacks, and use them to better yourself and be proud of the person you will become? Furthermore, I learnt *ask and you shall receive.*

Throughout my career as a professional medium I have had incredible experiences with spirit and their messages can only be described as mind-blowing, but I have also had opportunities to give random messages as well. Neither type of message is better: it is up to spirit and what they want to communicate and sometimes the random messages turn out to be more important. The session is always in spirits hands and trying to control the session is a mistake from the beginning. I believe I am only as good as the people I work with, if a loved one had random information to give in the session, that's all that will be given and if they wanted their loved one to be gob smacked with events that only they would know, they would give this information. I am not in control of what comes out of my mouth, I am only in control of how I deliver the information and random messages are just as important as the bells and whistle messages. Sometimes I never have any warning when your loved ones want to communicate with their family or friends they sometimes just pop in out of the blue and give me a message or show me a picture, that I have no clue about what I am looking at. But I have learnt just to say *thank you,* for the messages and all will be revealed when the time is right.

23

Guilt versus Regret

One of the subjects I discuss regularly in my readings is regrets. For many years I have told my clients:

"Never have regrets, because spirit doesn't have them." I was taught this by spirit at the beginning of my journey as a medium. But now as I am growing spiritually, spirit at times have said they do have regrets. This is not the case for every spiritual being I communicate with. However, I always thought that when we go to heaven, there would be no regrets that we have completed our lessons – although this is not always the case. Recently, I have been thinking about guilt and regrets more often, and after speaking with Rose and spirit I have a clearer understanding of this area of discussion.

I have read for many people throughout my career, and one thing I have noticed is that it is important for a loved one to say goodbye or say something that they believe will help their loved one cross over. If a person is not present when their loved one crosses over, there is tremendous guilt that is felt because they were not there at the end. If your loved one wanted you to be there, they would make sure you were there: it's like when you hear people say that their mother or father waited for a certain family member to travel to see them, and once they get there the person passes away. Sometimes our loved ones do not want us to see them take their last breath and they will wait until you leave the room to cross over. My grandfather did exactly that: I remember going to the hospital with my dad. After everyone said goodbye and that they would see him in the morning, and I was the only one left and when I said goodbye my grandfather looked me straight in the eye.

"See you later Jude." I knew then I would not see my grandfather alive again - something in his eyes that told me this was his way of saying goodbye and true to his word my grandfather did it his way. In my experience, if our loved ones do not want to say goodbye, then they will do it their way and cross over in their own time. When this happens, I often hear the lyrics - "I did it my way."

I believe guilt is felt when our soul connects to our conscious, telling it to say sorry or make some mends for something that we know we need to fix, and until we do we would feel a heavy burden on our shoulders. It is entirely up to us to try to rectify a situation, but once you have tried or admitted to the part you played, the guilt should be done.

24

Grief

People grieve in different ways

Being a medium, I spend a lot of time around grief. I see people grieve every day and what I have discovered, is grief is very personal. No-one can tell another person how to grieve. I am not an expert in this field, and I have never claimed to be, but what I know about grief is from experience and witnessing other people's grief. Before I wrote this chapter, I sat down and thought about what grief really means, my own experiences with it and how it had affected other people. I found I used my work as a platform to learn from other people. Grief can be experienced in so many ways: it can be a very debilitating experience and can be experienced by any sort of loss such as a death of a loved one, a loss of a job or a relationship, but my focus will be on the loss of a loved one.

There have been many books published on this topic, so I am not going to go into depth about grief, but I would like to talk about it from my point of view as a professional medium and my personal experiences. As a nurse, I saw a lot of ways people dealt with grief and the one thing I remember is that it was an individual experience. For instance, some people find relief in expressing themselves physically, such as wailing others may be in shock and their grief may not be felt until later when they had time to digest the situation. Some people may find it hard to express their emotions easily, whilst others will express their sadness openly. There may be feelings of anger and resentment, especially if a loved one had passed quickly or unexpectedly, and the person may want to blame something or someone and therefore ask the ask why, as their faith may be shattered for that moment. All emotions people may experience, I believe, make us stronger as a physical soul and it doesn't matter how long the grieving process take. I always say:

"*We will never get over our loved one's death, but we will learn to live,*"

People's reactions to death can be very different and just because a person isn't crying over a loved one passing, doesn't mean they aren't hurting. They may be still in shock or they may be a very private person and prefer to grieve in private. Another person may prefer to openly grieve in front of people, and there are other people where grief strikes suddenly because they may have thought about their loved one. What I have found is that no length of time could dissipate the grieving process. My friend Ronnie, whose mother I knew well, had passed whilst I was writing this book and she now contacts me regularly, especially when her family needs to hear from her. After the funeral, Ronnie had asked her mother to see me when she needed to hear from her. I was compelled to call Ronnie one day to see how she was, and when she answered, I knew there was something amiss. What I didn't know was that this day was close to her mother's birthday and she said she was shopping earlier before I called. She was fine and carrying on with her daily chores and out of the blue, something reminded her of her mother, Ronnie said she was walking to the shops and a woman walked passed her smoking a cigarette and her mum was a heavy smoker, she just stood in the grocery store and cried. Sometimes our emotions are overwhelming, the only way we can cope with grief is to go with our feelings.

Recently, I asked people on my private page to write about their experiences or their definition of what grief means to them. I was overwhelmed with their responses and blessed to have people write messages of personal experiences. I couldn't put everyone in this book, and I am grateful for everyone's contributions.

Emma

Hi, reader, my name is Emma and my dear friend Judy has asked me to write to a piece about grief and what it means to me.

Grief is a funny thing, such a small word with such a vast and different meaning to everyone. Some of you may remember my story from Jude's first book discussing the loss of my father at my engagement party. His passing is something I don't know I'll ever "get over." For me grief, is a very present word. I'll never be able to use the word 'grieved' as I feel it's never going to be something I refer to in the past tense. Not to say I'm wallowing or unable to live my life, but as I sit here thinking about what grief is to me, I can almost imagine it as a passenger on a bus. I know it's there; it may not be sitting in the front where I can see it, but every now and then when I look in the mirror I see it sitting quietly up the back and I'm reminded of its presence.

Thinking of my dad, I grieve his loss in my life, I miss his booming voice, his humour, his mannerisms, the way he loved my mother. He was a man who was dedicated to his family, not someone that said, "I love you" but showed his love in the things that he did.

I had a dream once (many years ago) where I heard a man singing. It was my dad and he came and stood in front of me. I began crying and hugged him, he looked at me smiling. I said, "are you staying?" He spoke no words, but just shook his head. I cried and didn't want to let him go. Thinking of that dream now, it still brings tears as I wish with all my heart he didn't have to leave.

And looking at my life now, almost eight years after his death, I now have three amazing children, which brings a different layer to his absence as I grieve the relationship, they will never get to have with him and that they all deserve. They'll never know what an amazing grandfather he would have been, how he would have always been there for them and boasted about them to his friends. Sometimes (as you can tell) I catch myself daydreaming about what could have been. At the end of the day I just miss him.

I've caught myself many times using the word 'unfair', when you grow up you learn about good vs. evil, fairness and doing the right thing. And yes, it does feel very unfair that he isn't here physically with us. And many times, I've asked the universe "why?" and no matter how many times you ask, there's never an answer that's good enough.

The love I feel for my dad will always be there, my children will know who he was through my stories of him and I'll tell them how he'll always love them and how proud he is of them and that he'll always be watching over them and no doubt whispering his all-knowing opinions in their ears.

And as Judy always says, "love never dies, it's a cord attached from their heart to yours."

I suppose the thing I try to remind myself is don't grieve because I lost, I grieve because I loved.

Love never dies.

Haley:

Haley spoke about how love cannot be measured, and neither can grief. There is no timeline, but it is an experience that we all go through. Everyone grieves differently, as I outlined earlier. In 2017 Hayley lost her husband's grandfather, who she considered a grandfather figure as well. Her husband, along with other family members carried their grandfather into the church and I remembered what the person conducting the service said:

"Grief is an honour,

Honour, that we loved, cared and knew that person so much that it is okay to hurt and to cry. To love is an honour and to grieve is an honour."

Hayley sat in the church and realised the truth in the statement, and It was an honour to be part of Pops life.

Over the years, Hayley has lost many people who were close to her, but the death of her nephew was most significant because he was only a baby and there was no explanation that she could accept when he died. As a result, her trust in faith was a daily struggle. However, through grief came spirituality and Haley recognised she was gaining a new spiritual understanding towards life and death, and we both learnt from grief.

Our suffering from grief is because of how much we love and care for one another, in the end we feel honoured to have loved and cared for our loved ones and they always take a piece of us with them to heaven.

Sandra

Sandra spoke about her grief over losing the person she cherished - her mother. She spoke about how grief is a silent word; nobody talks about and how someone's life can change from feeling light and carefree to dark and suffocating in an instant. The day her mum passed away felt surreal. Her whole world had changed forever because the person who was her world had gone. It was like a movie playing over and over, a dream and a nightmare rolled into one. The feeling of being trapped in this dream was overwhelming. All Sandra wanted to do when she buried her mum was to lie beside her.

Sandra couldn't accept she wouldn't be able to hug, hold or talk to her mother anymore. Nor could she just pick up the phone and call her mother to see how her day was or go and visit her mother when she felt like it and who would Sandra turn to when she needed advice? There were a lot of emotions she had to go through: feeling angry and confused she frequently asked:

"How could she do this to me?" She wanted to scream for the world to stop moving, because other people getting on with their lives and the world was moving forward, while she was dying and frozen in the same place.

People are educated in many areas, but we as physical beings will never be prepared completely, when grief occurs. It is said that time heals all wounds, but for Sandra, no time will help her heal from her mother's passing. She said it is

"A hole in her heart that will never close," and she misses her mother more each day. I hope one-day Sandra's heart will heal.

Keira spoke of the need to be kind to the people who are grieving, because nobody really knows how much another person is hurting. People might be standing next to a person who is completely broken, and they wouldn't even know, so be kind because you never know who you might be standing next to.

After reading everyone's contributions, I realised the key point discussed was how grief is an individual thing: no-one has the right to tell you how to grieve. Grief can be more than an emotion; it sometimes can be a state of being or an existence. The feeling can be raw and strong, it has longevity that seems to last a lifetime, but it can change in its appearance. I have said previously, individuals will never get over a loved one passing, but they are encouraged to learn to live, because at the end of the day, do you want to construct a wall in front of your loved ones when you go home because you couldn't move forward? Or do you want to learn to live, and be free without limitations but still miss them? Of course, it is okay to grieve for our loved ones because we were honoured to love and know them. They will stay in our hearts for ever.

I was asked a question recently by a friend, "Do spirit grieve for their loved ones here in the physical, and what emotions do they feel towards their loved one's grief?". It was a great question and one I had never pondered, because talking to spirit and bringing them through is so natural to me. In my experience, when I see spirit, they are happy and healthy in heaven and it is important to let their loved ones know they are happy and healthy in heaven, especially if the their loved one had suffered from an illness before they crossed over. Spirit does feel the grief of their loved ones in the physical and I have cried on many occasions in a reading or platform, because spirit will show their emotion by crying. Spirit cries because of a beautiful memory they want their loved one to remember and the love I feel from spirit towards their loved one is indescribable.

I remember reading for a group of people at a platform, and a young man came through and asked me to give a message to his wife in the audience. I found her and asked if her husband had recently passed from an illness. She said her husband had just recently passed from cancer, leaving behind herself and their small child.

The lady's husbands' message was:

"I didn't get to say l love you, before I died".

The lady replied "yes, he didn't get to say he loved me before he died". At this point, I could feel the love he had for his wife and I knew the message he had for her was so important to him. I couldn't stop the tears from falling when I relayed his response to his wife, he said:

"I have come through now to tell you, I love you".

There wasn't a dry eye in the audience, I knew he was watching over his wife and small child, and it was important for him to tell his wife he loved her because he knew she was grieving over this.

This story illustrates, how spirit grieves, and when it is the right time, they will choose someone to communicate and deliver a message from their heart to their loved one's heart, just like this husband communicated his love for his wife.

25

The Power of Prayer

Mother Teresa once wrote *"Prayer is putting oneself in the hands of God, at His dispositions, and listening to His voice in the depths of our hearts."*

Before I started to write this chapter, *The Power of Prayer,* I sat down and thought what prayer really means to me and how is it significant in my life. Do I pray daily or only when its necessary? Do I know what prayer really means or am I doing it correctly? I began to watch how other people pray, including at churches or in the privacy of their own homes. One day I was sitting out the back of my home in our newly constructed sitting area near our pool, and I heard my neighbour at the back of my house chanting and I recognised he was maybe praying or performing his religious ritual: some religions take moments throughout the day to kneel and pray.

I realised my comprehension of prayer and praying was limited, and that it didn't matter - what did matter was what I believed prayer to be. I summed it up as talking to God, or whoever you believe in. It is having a private conversation with a religious being and it doesn't matter, if it was a formal text or what your heart says. Many people pray on a regular basis and some pray intermittently. I believe there is no official way but if the person does it from a pure intention that's the right way. This is not to say I am an expert on how to pray or that I know the true definition of it.

Every day I use formal prayer to start my day, and to help to enhance the energy and protection in my house before I see clients. It's not enough just to say the words to a prayer, we must believe in what we are saying with clear intentions. If not, they become just words on a page. This daily ritual happens every day before I start the work I love to do. I say my prayers for protection, clear guidance and bringing spirit through. Recently, my routine was feeling forced, and because I was tired, it felt like it was becoming a chore. I would say the words and they felt they didn't have any meaning to them. Until I sat and really read the words I was saying. I was too busy thinking about each reading and how I thought the day would go, instead of leaving it to spirit as they always know best. I was trying to take control instead of handing it over to spirit. Once this was brought to my attention from spirits and an Angels gentle nudge, I went back and re visited each prayer and read it with clear intention. Not because I had too, but because I wanted too.

I decided to include true stories in this chapter and to demonstrate, how prayer is real, and God and the Archangels always hear, and our prayers and are answered in the right time. My Aunty Janet, my godmother, wrote in my Bible when I was a little girl and said: just remember when you pray, keep it simple, there are no right or wrong ways to pray, if your words come from your heart you cannot go wrong.

In 2017, one of my children asked if they could go to a friend's house and sleep overnight. I decided they could go, but we needed to know the name and the address of their friend. Darrin dropped them off. "Have they given you the details?" I asked him.

I dropped them off with their friends at the shops and from there, they would be going to their friends house and they said they would text us the address." We didn't receive the text message, and we knew then they forgot to message us. That night, Darrin and I decided to sit the and watch television. But still I couldn't shake the feeling that there would be a text message asking me to come and get our child. A moment later, I had an overwhelming feeling to check my mobile phone, even though I had checked it two minutes earlier. I noticed I had a missed call from them and when I phoned them, there was no answer. I called a couple of times to see what they wanted, and it went straight to voice mail. Then I received another text message asking me to come and get them. Instantly, I knew my instincts were right, call it a mother's perception, but it was a feeling of hopelessness because I didn't know where to pick them up from because I didn't have an address along with. I didn't have their phone number programmed into Find a Friend mobile app. I started to panic when the next message said:

"Please come and get me, I'm not feeling well." Darrin could see the panic in my face.

"What's up?"

"Something is wrong."

We both tried separately to call them on our phones, with no answer, they replied twenty minutes later, which felt like a lifetime of worry and said, they wanted to come home. But the problem was, we didn't have an address to go to. Darrin messaged for at least a half an hour without a reply and at this stage, I was a wreck and we began to argue because we didn't know the address or phone number of the family they were staying at and I knew my child wouldn't like to impose on the family they were staying with by telling them they didn't feel well, so I guessed the family didn't know. I felt I was living in my worst nightmare and all rational thoughts went out the window. I stood in my bedroom with tears in my eyes and a moment later, an overwhelming feeling of comfort and love encompassed me, and I heard very clearly:

"Pray to Archangel Michael," so I kneeled before my bed and started to pray and asked for guidance from Archangel Michael. Ten minutes later, Darrin walked into the room:

"They have finally responded and given us the address." In that second, I knew, everything was going to be okay and Archangel Michael had heard my prayer, I was never alone.

We drove to their friend's house and our child said they felt sick because they must have eaten something that didn't agree with them and they didn't want to tell their friend's parents they were sick. All kinds of thoughts went through my head as we drove home about what might have happened if we weren't guided by Archangel Michael and there were so many emotions I was feeling: anger, frustration and relief. This night out taught me a lesson: when a situation is out of your control, the power of prayer is important because God and the Angels will guide you even if you don't know where you are going. Also from a practical viewpoint, to insist your children to give you the details of where they are staying before they leave the house.

The second story I heard from a beautiful lady named Louise. She was one of my very first clients when I started mediumship professionally. I met Louise ten years ago and gave her a reading at her daughter's house. I was new to this and, I didn't realise the impact spirit's words would have on my clients. I remember talking to Louise about her loved ones in spirit and halfway through the reading, I felt the presence of Jesus. Because I have seen him most of my life, I didn't realise the words he was saying were that important. As I communicated the message, I remember hesitating and questioning what I had to say. Then an overwhelming feeling came over me and the words just poured out. I said that Louise would be involved in an accident; it wasn't her fault, and someone would unfortunately pass. I continued to say that this wasn't her fault, the events of the accident were meant to happen because this was the way it was supposed to be, and to know Jesus would be there by her side and helping her get through this. A week after the reading, I received a telephone call from Louise's daughter. Two days after her mum came for her reading, she was driving safely down a mountain road where she lived and out of nowhere, a motorcycle appeared right in front of Louise. She didn't have any warning or time to stop the car before the accident happened, and the young man was killed. At that point I was speechless. I went and spoke to Darrin immediately and when I was finished talking to Darrin, I finished with:

"I'm not doing any readings anymore." A few days later Louise heard about my decision to leave my work and phoned me to reassure me it wasn't my fault: the accident was meant to happened and that I was only the messenger. The police investigated the accident and concluded that it wasn't her fault either. Louise stressed that I had to continue to read because if it wasn't for the messages from Jesus, she would not have coped with what happened, and before she finished our conversation she said " at the time of the accident, she felt Jesus with her, before and after the incident and this gave her strength."

Recently, Louise came for another reading and this was the first time I had seen her since the accident. We talked after the reading, and Louise told me a story of how her prayers were answered.

For six months after the accident she would pray to God for the young man's family and for forgiveness from them. She asked for a sign to know if her prayers had been answered and they were. Louise and her daughter were talking one day, and she talked about what happened in a coffee shop her friend works in.

The friend was busy serving customers, and a man walked into the coffee shop and ordered a coffee. This man was the deceased man's friend and they both would come into the coffee shop on a regular basis to order their coffees. Whilst the barrister was making the man's coffee, she made reference to his friend and said she hadn't seen him for a while and the man replied his friend had died at an intersection on his motor bike, six months ago. The man went onto say that he wished he could tell the driver of the other car, that there were no hard feelings towards them, and that the family of the deceased, were doing okay.

As they were talking, the barrister noticed her friend, Louise's daughter walking past the shop and she said:

"Funny you should say that, the young girl walking past the shop, is the other driver's daughter and will pass on the message." Louise's prayers were answered, and this was a beautiful example of how the power of prayer and believing in your prayers would be answered when it was the right time and right place. Thank you, Louise for sharing your story and it was a beautiful illustration of how prayers do really get heard and answered at the right time.

The last story is my own experience with the power of prayer and the presence of Mother Mary. My son graduated from a Catholic high school and in the evening, I was asked to attend their graduation mass.

"I have to go to church," I said to Rose, and I really wasn't in the mood to go.

"Just go, because you might experience or learn something," Rose said to me. The night went smoothly, and funnily enough I did enjoy myself. I remember thinking to myself whilst I was listening to the priest give his address of how my week had been dreadful, and I was worried about my son taking his exams in the next few weeks. I had been praying to Mother Mary for weeks and asking for her guidance because I know she helps with children and parenting.

The time came when everyone received the blessing of Christ. I contemplated receiving the body of Christ, but because I have been christened Church of England, I thought it was disrespectful to receive the Eucharist. The priest did offer a blessing as well, and I considered it but chickened out. It was nearing the end of this ceremony, and as I was sitting there, an intense rose smell washed over me. I immediately looked around to see if a person was standing next to me with rose perfume on. But no one was standing next to or near me to explain the smell. At that moment an overwhelming feeling of peace washed over me. I knew without a doubt Mother Mary was answering my prayers. In my experience, roses or flowers smells confirm

Mother Mary is around when we need her. Whilst I was procrastinating about whether or not to go to the priest and obtain blessing, I recognised the lesson spirit wanted me to learn at that moment, although we celebrate different religions, we are all God's children and are worthy to receive a sanctification.

26

We Are Never Alone

I am sure everyone has heard the phrase; you are never alone. It is a well-known expression used in songs and in books all the time. When I was young, I used to hear this all the time, and I didn't know how profound it would be in my life and in the importance of it in my work.

I always knew I was never alone because I have always felt the presence of Angels, God, Jesus and spirit. But, like a lot of people there are things we experience in our lives where our faith can be tested. We believe we are alone, and have no-one to talk to, or feel like people don't understand what we are going through. I am sure you can identify with this emotional state at least one time in your life.

In my first book, *The Voice of Spirit*, I talked about my childhood and at times how hard it was to fit in with other children, family and friends. I mentioned a tragic incident I went through at the age of five. It was the first time I felt my Angels around me. It was from that time forth I knew of my Angels presence always. As an adult my faith falters, but when I collect my thoughts and centre myself, I become focused. Having faith isn't always easy: I have to practice it every day. The days I don't know where to turn or if the path is unclear for me I give it to God and say I let go and let God, because that's all I can do without becoming frustrated and wanting to take control of things that are out of my control. In other words, I am trying to avoid becoming a control freak.

In my profession I have tried to control what happens in a session without giving it to spirit. I have seen firsthand what spirit is capable of and the information they bring through is so precise, only their loved one could know about it. I want everyone to experience it. See how I said I want: I have experienced many times in my career, that what I want and expect spirit to do in a session is totally different to what happens, and the information is always for my client's interest. I am aware my sessions are not for me to control. Because the information is from spirit, they are in control and how it is delivered.

I have seen many situations involving a miracle or marvel and I know that there is no explanation for it, other than an act of God or a sign from spirit. It could be a small or large phenomenon, it doesn't matter: the signs are there. As a result, when I use the phrase you are not alone in my sessions, I am serious. Recently, my sister-in-law, Teneal asked me to watch a movie that was released in 2017 called The Shack. It is the story about a family tragedy, and how a father blamed God for what happened, until he met God, Jesus and another spiritual being his questions were answered.

"Why does God allow bad things to happen?" I cannot explain how the movie answered this question, as I don't think I would do it justice, so you will have to watch the movie. Nevertheless, while the father was talking to these heavenly beings, the one saying that stood out for me was you are never alone. This movie had a huge impact on me because throughout the movie I could relate to many spiritual scenes and related phrases. One example was a scene where children play in heaven, this was a nice validation. The second scene triggered a memory when I performed one of my first events in front of an audience.

Every time I have an event and I am in front of an audience, I become nervous and anxious. My belief in spirit is so great, and I am anxious to get out there and tell people what spirit is about, along with the messages for their loved ones. Before a show, I must sit quietly and be with spirit, centre myself with the help of Rose, my spiritual healer and dear friends who helps me on the night. I must trust spirit without reservation and believe in what I am saying. Before I start, I meditate and ask spirit to come forward after I ask God, Jesus, my Angels, Spirit Guides, Helpers and other divinities to come forward. I can feel them advancing, because I feel hot sensations over my body, and cold sensations on my legs. I feel tingles when my Angels are near, and a blanket being placed over me. Therefore, I know I am never alone and trust in spirit.

To prepare for an event, I schedule a healing session with my incredible healer and friend, Stacy. When the sessions start, I have the habit of going out of my body. I remember floating to heaven once. Through the clouds, where everything became white, I had the feeling of being free and incredibly loved. As I was standing on what looked like a cloud, a bright light descended upon me and it was so striking it made me cry. As I blinked back the tears, I saw spirits of families I had previously read for, my family and relations of people I was yet to bring through. It was the most amazing sight I have ever experienced. They were all standing together in many lines around me. There was a beautiful glow to each spirit, and they looked so youthful and peaceful. The feeling was overwhelming and the image before me was exactly what the movie portrayed. I remember crying in my healing session because the love that emanated from spirit in front of me was indescribable and a blessing. At the time, my husband's uncle and aunty had died in the same year. Their daughter was attending my event the next day. Darrin's Uncle Warwick was in front of the line of spirits and he said he was fine and to give his daughter a kiss from him and when I saw her at the show, I gave her the message and a kiss from her dad.

It's funny, The Shack, described the father's purpose for meeting God and the heavenly beings focussed on his individual healing, he was given a glimpse by God of spirits standing exactly how I saw them. The message I received from spirit in my healing session with Stacy was you are never alone. Sometimes we need reminding that we are never alone; our loved ones and heavenly beings are always with us even though we cannot always feel or hear them. Just because we can't see something doesn't mean it is not there. Spirit will always try to give you signs when the time is appropriate, and it is up to us to notice these signs. Remember, signs can be subtle or in your face, but mostly the occurrences you cannot describe are from spirit.

One of the things I have learnt from being a medium is that my trust in God, Jesus and other heavenly beings has been strengthened. Their love feeds the soul. Before a reading, I ask for Gods wisdom to guide me, Jesus's light to shine through me and my Angels to help me. However, after watching the movie, it highlighted the importance of knowing we are never alone in our everyday lives. The times we feel abandoned, confused or unloved are the times we should know that these unseen and heavenly beings are watching over, guiding us and walking with us on our journey - we are never alone.

27

Knowing the Right Time to Communicate with Spirit

My spiritual journey has had many lessons and learning for spiritual growth. This journey has been quite rewarding, gratifying and truly amazing.

As I have previously discussed, knowing the right time to communicate with spirit is important and, in my experience, you cannot force a loved one to talk to you just because you are ready. There are other factors to consider: for instance, if a person has been unwell for a long time, when they cross over into heaven, they may need to visit the healing room - this is about healing their soul and enhancing their vibration. This is equally important for a person who died tragically. If you think about it, when you are sick, your energy or vibration is dull or unresponsive compared to our usual self. Therefore, to restore this vibration, we need some healing, and this is done through the healing room. Another reason why they might not come through in a reading might be because the family isn't ready. This does not mean they won't come through ever, there might be a block standing in their way such as grief or a person wanting their loved ones to materialise in front of them or do something only their loved one would do. One thing I do know about spirit is that they do not like to be told what they are to do so they will not jump through hoops, so to speak just in because you have asked them to do it. I work on this scenario: if a person was not overly enthusiastic in life, they may not be overly enthusiastic spirit.

However, I have had on some occasions during a reading had a loved one that was expressive and very communicative, but in life was very quiet. I remember a family member who is very quiet and reserved, but when he had a couple of drinks you could not shut him up. I had a whole conversation with them at a family gathering for the first time, and I had known them all of their life. I am not saying that it only takes a drink for spirit to communicate, but spirit has taught me that anything can happen in a reading and it is awesome when it does.

In May 2019, Bec came to see me for a reading. She has been a regular client since her mum passed away. It had been two years since I had seen her, and the minute she walked into my reading room, I saw a man standing in the corner waiting for her. I started the reading and the man said:

"I am here to speak to Rebecca, and would you sing Happy Birthday to her for me please".

I was surprised at his comment and reluctant to sing happy Birthday, because I am not a great singer and his energy felt he had only passed recently. I asked Bec, if a man had passed recently and if she could understand Happy Birthday and how he referred to her as Rebecca and not Bec. She started to cry and said

"The man is my father, he only died five weeks ago, and it is my birthday today". "My dad never called me Bec! He hated it!"

The reading began and Bec's father didn't disappoint, Bec could validate information her father was conveying. At one point, I stopped the reading because I could hear a bell ringing continuously in my head and when I asked Bec about a bell she didn't understand the message at first. The ringing continued and I asked Bec again, if she could take this information. At that point, her father showed me something being placed in his top pocket and I thought this was an item someone else put in his pocket after he had passed away. I relayed this information to Bec the best way I could, and at that moment, my doorbell rang and when we went to investigate and see who was at the door, no one was there.

We went back into my reading room, sat down and Bec became so excited, because she remembered what the ringing bell meant. Bec said:
"She was her father's carer for the past few years, and prior to him moving in with her, he lived by himself. Bec would get worried about her father and in case of an emergency, Bec bought a wireless doorbell. He would keep the ringer in his pocket and press it when he needed Bec. A doorbell sound would chime in her house when he pressed the button. What's more, Bec had put the remote control in his pocket for safe keeping"

To say I was blown away, was an understatement. For Bec's dad to show me putting something in his pocket and then ringing my doorbell to help Bec to understand what he was saying, was amazing. We both laughed and cried during the reading, but we were very grateful for her father's presence. This was a great example of spirit knew the right time to communicate with their loved one.

As I have previously said, spirit will always come through when it is the right time and believe me, I will know about it long before my clients will.

Something to think about. If you ever find yourself in a position of wanting to communicate with your loved ones in heaven, say to yourself:

"When the time is right, you will know?" *Well that's a bit cryptic.* One thing I do know about spirit, is that spirit will make it happen when it's supposed to happen.

At times, spirit is reluctant to come through for a family member, because of the way they have crossed over, and in my experience, this is to do with suicide. Spirit always know what we are feeling because they feel it them selves and if a person coming for a reading is angry with their loved one in spirit, spirit will be reluctant to come through. When this happens, I am honest with my client and explain the situation and most of the time, after I have explained myself, the client's energy changes, and I am able to bring through their loved one. Once the client accepts my explanation and the way their loved one died, the energy changes and the image I see of spirit goes from looking cloudy to a much more clearer image and the barrier my client may have unintentionally put up dissipates, and the reading is more fluent.

What I have learnt from spirit is that when they are ready to communicate with their loved ones depends on how evolved their soul is. If they are an old soul and they have done this before, they would communicate and come through in a reading quickly. I have had a person come through within twelve hours of crossing over. If you are a new soul, then the transition of communicating with their loved ones may take a little while. In both cases spirit will know when it is the right time to communicate.

Part Two

28

Memorable Short Stories about Connections With Our Loved Ones Who Have Crossed Over

Throughout my career as a medium, I have been blessed with the ability to communicate with loved ones who have passed over, and to help them connect with their family or friends here on earth. I consider this to be a miracle. The wonder is not just communicating with spirit, but in the validation and confirmation of events they ask me to relay to their loved ones.

In any case, I believe it is a privilege to be chosen as the communicator between Heaven and Earth. I would like to share some stories of how spirit has connected to their loved ones to help them find peace in their life on Earth. To do this, they tell their loved ones they have successfully transitioned into Heaven and are still in constant communication with family and friends.

Before I start, I would like to thank all of the people who gave me permission to share their accounts of how spirit would confirm to them that there is life after life. I am honoured to be the one who connects us to the spirit world. A big thank you also to the spirits who allowed me to write their stories. I hope that by reading these stories, you may find peace knowing that we are not alone and that there is life after life. These are the stories of how love is eternal. It was important to me to document some of these remarkable spirit stories. I hope you enjoy their gentle humour and feel the love they bring from Heaven.

While not an expert on the subject, when it comes to grief and how we cope with the death of a loved one, I believe it helps to know that the loved one in spirit is happy and their soul continues to live on in Heaven.

To everyone who has allowed me to tell their story, it is with much gratitude that I share them here. I thank you from the bottom of my heart for allowing me this great privilege.

Judy x

Note: for the purpose of this book, I have changed some names to protect the identity of the kind people who have generously agreed to allow me to share their stories. Please take these personal stories as messages from your loved ones in spirit and know that love is forever.

29

The Gift of Life

I am sure everyone or I hope everyone, has had a moment in their life or career, where they have had the wow factor! In my career as a medium, I have had experienced something monumental, and I was thunderstruck, and from this, it has had a huge impact on my life.

I was preparing for a reading with a lady named Lauren. Whilst I was getting organised; I could feel a young man just standing to my right. He was waiting for my client to come in for her reading. The minute Lauren sat down, he stood to her right and was waiting to be introduced to her. I described him as a young male between the ages of eighteen to twenty years of age, and he had passed away in a car accident. He mentioned organ donations. Lauren was stunned for a moment but knew exactly who he was and what he was communicating. I worked out his name to start with a K or a C and he wanted to get a message to his mother to let her know that he was okay. Lauren was amazed at the information he was delivering, and she could relate to it all. Even though Lauren didn't know this young man personally, she said would contact his mother and pass on the message.

A few months later a client named Shelley, came to see me. Originally, the appointment was for Lauren, but at the last minute the appointment was given to Shelley. She travelled over three hours to come her appointment. I had no idea who Shelley was, and initially I thought she was Lauren's mother because I knew there was a strong connection. As soon as Shelley sat down, I noticed the same young man from Lauren's reading was there. He was standing next to Shelley, and I felt he was closely connected to Shelley. I wasn't sure why he was here, but I mentioned him to Shelley, and she said that he was her son named Kaden and he passed away in a car accident.

Kaden said he was seventeen and had just got his license. He was in a car accident and there was someone in the car with him - Kaden's elder brother was in the car with him. He continued to say he was on the way to a job - this meant he was on his way to his Nan's place to remove the leaves from her gutters, five minutes from his home.

He said he had good brains and was preparing to do his Higher School Certificate and go onto University.

"This is all true," Shelley replied. Sometimes in a reading, my own life has parallels with another client. At that moment I could resonate with Kaden's story because at the same time my own son was seventeen years old, had just received his licence and he was also doing his Higher School Certificate.

Kaden loved life. He was a fun-loving boy who loved all people. Shelley said it was all true and he was loved by everyone he met. Kaden went on to talk about the Red Cross and blood, Shelley told me her family had been holding a blood drive each year, as a positive way to remember his passing. Kaden wanted to bring up his little sister. He said she would go to bed every night with her teddy bear and talk to him. When Shelley went home and told her ten-year-old daughter about the teddy bear, her daughter just cried. She told her mother every night she would go to bed with her teddy bear and talk to Kaden, even though she hadn't met him because Shelley was pregnant with her daughter at the time of his accident. Shelley sent me a message later saying that she did not know this and that her daughter had been doing this before she went to bed all her life.

He also brought up a new cologne that his brother had bought, and a trip overseas- his family was going to America. When I told Shelley this, she was surprised and said it was unlikely they would go. Kaden's brother who lives overseas had recently bought a new cologne and spoke to his mum after the reading to tell her about it. Shelley contacted me later via email.

"A special lady once told me that I would be having a holiday in America this year and I said, I don't think so, I hate planes. Well, a few months after that, one of my sons moved to America, so guess who I am going to visit these school holidays for 6 weeks."

Spirits will often talk about their funerals, and it always amazes me, how humble they are and excited to see all their family and friends and Kaden wasn't any different. He said

"My funeral was huge" and his mother responded, he had around 800 people attend his funeral and I could understand this through the beautiful energy he was emanating.

The moment I met Kaden in my first reading with Lauren, I knew he was special, and I was to go through a life changing event. Whist Shelley was authenticating Kaden's messages, I paused for a moment.

"Did you donate his organs" and Shelley replied yes. Kaden showed me his eyes.

"They were the only organs they did not donate."

"He was happy to help," he said and at that moment I wasn't sure what he meant. He gave me the letter D, and Shelley looked shocked, because a man called David was a recipient of his heart.

"Mum it beats."

"We know it does, because we are in touch with David."

The biggest shock of all was finding out Lauren, the lady I previously read for, was a recipient of his kidneys and pancreas.

"She would have died, mum." He was referring to Lauren who would have died had she not received his organs when she did. Over the years, Kaden sends messages for or about Lauren through Shelley's readings, and it is my absolute pleasure to communicate for Kaden.

After Kaden's organs were donated, there was a lot of publicity about him.

"I'm famous," Kaden said. He wanted to reassure his mum he was still watching over her and sending his love, he mentioned

"Someone cut my hair."

"I cut a lock of his hair after the organ donation."

After the reading, we sat for a while and talked about some of the messages, she was able to confirm. There were some that she didn't know at the time, but some she could.

"I kept quiet because I wanted to hear what Kaden had to say and if I could validate his messages." Believe me, she didn't give me anything and I was happy with this because I believe this is all spirits messages and I am just a communicator.

The most amazing part of the reading was when Shelley told me of how she booked an appointment for a reading. She asked me if I remembered Lauren and her reading? I said I remember Lauren, and Kaden had come through in her reading. Shelley said that Lauren had contacted her after the reading to relay the message Kaden had given her for his mother. She continued to say Lauren didn't know Kaden personally because she was the recipient of his organs and when he came through, she knew it was important for his mum to listen to the CD.

I realized that I was a part of something incredible. I cannot describe the feeling I had, it was a privilege to be Kaden's voice. To speak to the donor and recipient in one reading was astonishing, and an incredible honour and there are no words to describe how I felt to help bring three people together through Kaden's love. Kaden touched so many lives when he was alive and was adored by many. He has now touched so many more from spirit and through his act of kindness and selflessness that made the people who received his organs have fulfilling lives filled with love.

I want to say huge thank you to Kaden for choosing me to communicate his messages and how he has reinforced, that there is truly life after life, and that from an amazing soul, a gift of life was given to another soul.

A Mothers Love

When people know I am a professional medium, they sometimes expect me to know everything, especially because of my link to the spirit world. They believe I have direct knowledge of when someone will pass. Before any reading, I outline what people can expect from the reading and something I outline concerns the passing of a loved one on Earth. I state that it isn't my job to tell people when they are about to cross over. This is up to God, and because I am not God, I do not know everything. In simple terms, I am not allowed to say when someone will pass. If I do receive a message when someone is passing, I tell my client to spend as much time with their loved one as they can and to create memories and experiences and tell them you love them. My next story is close to my heart because it involves a close friend and the love he shared with his mother.

Throughout, the year, I travel to different places giving readings to various people in various events, and I have close friends and family, who always give up their time to come and help me and I cannot thank them enough for their love and support, I also, meet beautiful people at my events and they offer to help. One of these people is my friend Anthony. Last year, he and his partner, James travelled to a show I was having down south from where we live. Before the show, I always prepare myself, and this night I had my mentor and friend Rose with me. She was giving me healing before I started. Anthony came to say hello and wish me good luck, and immediately I saw this grey haze around him.

He looked tired, and or flat. I immediately asked if he was okay, and he said he was fine. Something was still nagging at me, and I asked him several times after that if something was wrong. It got the point where Rose said to me to stop asking as him, because he said he was fine and that he just won some money on the poker machine, so nothing was wrong.

I started my night and delivered messages from spirit, but I remember saying that I had a gentleman in spirit, who loved betting on horses. No-one could really confirm this. At the end of the night, Anthony mentioned that he recognised the information, because his mum's uncle loved horse racing, and loved to bet. When he was playing the pokies, he asked if they could come through to help him win, and he did. He continued to say he felt his family around him that night especially. I also mentioned on numerous occasions the sign of a cross that I could see.

The next day I called the boys from the car to thank them for the night, and they mentioned they were heading up the coast to go and have lunch with Anthony's parents. Anthony was extremely close to his parents especially his mother, Elizabeth. After I ended the call, I still didn't shake the feeling something was happening, and it was out of my control. The week before my event, I thought of my Aunty Shirley often, who lived up the coast and I didn't know why. When we got home, I received a phone call from James telling us that Elizabeth had been rushed to hospital and ten minutes later he called back to say she had passed away. We dropped everything and travelled to the hospital.

We were greeted by James, and when I met up with Anthony, the first thing he asked me was:

"Why didn't you tell me she was going to die?" I was taken back for a moment, because this was the first time, I had a close friend ask me this question. I said I wasn't supposed to know. I knew then why I had the premonition, but it was out of my control. I felt helpless and I knew this was a lesson for me. To see someone, you care about hurting so much was heart wrenching, and I knew being there was the best thing I could do.

As we sat in the hospital, I realised the messages I was receiving the night before all made sense. The hospital we were at was the same hospital my Aunty Shirley was in before she passed away. The street the hospital was built on had something to do with horse racing, and I knew why Anthony's family were close last night. The visions of crosses I had become evident when we were dropping someone home to Anthony's parents' house. As we were coming over a crest, right in front of me was a massive cross.

That night, I couldn't sleep. I kept thinking of my two friends, and I felt Anthony's mum sit next to me.

"Tell Anthony I love him and that I have made it." I didn't know what to do, because I didn't want to disturb him as it was late. The decision was taken out if my hands moments later when I received a call from Anthony. He apologised for the late call, but he wanted to ask me a question.

"I just want to know if mum has made it to heaven and that she is okay." I was so thankful I could give his mum's message. We talked for a while and Elizabeth was so strong: she said to tell him that she supported a football team called the Bulldogs and Anthony replied she did go for the Bulldogs. At that moment, my husband Darrin walked into the room wearing a Bulldog's shirt. We talked, and I felt so blessed that Elizabeth chose me to give her message to her son.

I was scheduled to do another event, and Darrin and I decided to dedicate the show to Elizabeth's memory. We held it at her favourite place. At our nights, we have raffle prizes and the money is donated to a charity. My mother-in-law always helps with these and makes gorgeous hampers to give away. I found out was that she works for the store that Elizabeth loved to shop at and was a frequent customer. Some of the prize's my mother-in-law gave us to raffle off was a sewing machine and a basket of soaps, shampoos and other toiletries. On the day of the event, Anthony called me, and I told him about the prizes I had to raffle. He just laughed.

"Mum loved to go to buy material to make clothes and loved her sewing machine." When Anthony's dad was going through Elizabeth's belongings, he noticed that she bought so much soap, shampoo and conditioner. But the one thing that amazed both Anthony and myself, was that his dad was going through some books, and he put a pile to the side and asked Anthony to have a look and see if he wanted any of them. When he looked at the pile, my first book was on top of the pile. He didn't know that Elizabeth had bought my book. As I was driving, I could hear Elizabeth and she was telling me about seafood. When I mentioned this to Anthony, he said he was going to lunch with his family and will see what they have on menu. Sure enough, one of his family members had seafood for lunch.

The night was great fun, and Elizabeth didn't disappoint. I remember, I singled out Anthony and said that he was picked to perform in front of a crowd and in the presence of a star. He just smiled at me. He said, he had just been notified he was going to perform on television in front of a famous person and no-one knows about it.

"Well, mum wanted this audience to know how proud she is of you."

I have always had the privilege to be Anthony's grandmother's voice and she always lets me know when to give him a message. I am honoured to be Elizabeth's voice, and I have had many conversations and visitations from her because she has quite a strong energy, particularly when I am in a reading with a client and she pops in to give me a message. When my client cannot take my message, I know it's for Anthony. I must admit that I love spirit and I look forward to hearing from Elizabeth. She is always so proud of her children and grandchildren.

It never surprises me the love that emanates from a love one in heaven for their family members here on Earth. I am so blessed to be the communicator between Heaven and Earth, and the love Anthony and Elizabeth share is priceless, and it will last forever.

Luca

As a professional medium, you meet so many wonderful people and their stories touch your heart in so many ways, especially when it involves a child. The unconditional love they have for their family here on Earth, the love that embraces two people and unites their souls is remarkable. The next story is an example of the infinite love a mother has for her baby son. Communicating with children who have passed is particularly poignant for me, and it is always a privilege to bring them through to speak with their families. Having the opportunity to be their voice is immensely gratifying.

I wanted to share this story with you about a baby boy named Luca and how he came through to communicate with his mother Rosa. The events leading up to our meeting were orchestrated twice by him and he answered Rosa's prayers. This story is written through Rosa's eyes and I hope you appreciate, as much as I have, the bond between a parent and child is never-ending and our children in heaven will always present opportunities for us to receive the signs. Love never dies.

To help me connect with a client, their loved ones give me initials, whether it is for their first name, last name or a person here on Earth: their name is linked to the person in spirit. This was the case with a little baby boy called Luca. During one week of readings I asked all my clients:

"Who is Lucas, please?" and no-one knew this name or little boy. This happens quite often; I say to my clients:

"I look like the idiot, but as long as I find the person, it is okay." People are excited to talk to their loved ones in heaven. The confirmation that they are still around us is priceless. Spirit gets excited to talk to their family as well, and sometimes they hang around me until I talk to their loved one here on earth. I remember having a child named Nicholas with me in every reading for month, and I had asked all my clients if they knew this child. Nobody did. It wasn't until at the end of the month when a woman came for a reading and after I asked her about Nicholas, she said he was her nephew and he was excited to see her and validated his presence.

I was visiting Rose, and I mentioned what had happened with Luca, and how I was getting frustrated that I couldn't find the person, because I knew he had to give a special message to his mother and family. Rose encouraged me to keep going and be patient, because I would find the person I was looking for. I was scheduled to perform at a church on that weekend and the minute I walked into the church, I was drawn to a lady siting in the audience I had not met before. I knew I had to talk to her, but I didn't know why. I started my platform in front of the audience and after a little while I went to a lady sitting on her own. I saw a little baby sitting next to her. I asked if she knew the name Lucas, and she replied:

"I have a son Luca, and he died two months ago. He was premature, and my name is Rosa."

"Thank God I have found the right person, because he has been trying to get my attention all week."

Luca Joe Silvestri Arena was born the third of February 2015 and passed away on the seventh of February 2015. Rosa and her fiancé, Vince, were so excited to be having the baby they had been longing for. While Rosa was pregnant, she would always hear the song *My Name is Luka*, and when Luca passed, they hardly ever heard the song, except when they had been out for the day and it was the first song that was played on the radio.

Luca was born prematurely and the night he was born, when Rosa was trying to get some sleep, a white cloud with big googly eyes in the shape of the Michelin man from the television tyre advertisement years ago hovered over her head. Rosa looked at the cloud.

"Go away, you are not taking him, you cannot take him." Then the next day her fiancé, Vince, said:

"The doctors want a meeting with us, because it's not good news." Rosa immediately knew, what she had seen the previous night meant Luca was quite sick and the cloud was a premonition from spirit. I felt it was so important for Luca to describe his last moments with his mother, he showed me, he was lying in an incubator crib in the NICU, and Luca opened one eye to look at his mother. I asked Rosa, if she remembered this moment and she said

"Yes, I remember that. I asked him, if he wanted his dad and I to fight for him or to let him go? He wanted to be let go, as he was tired."

The day of Luca's funeral, Rosa and Vince returned home, and Rosa sat outside and looked up to the sky and she saw an amazing sight. A flock of birds were flying together in an L shape formation. Instantly, Rosa knew her baby boy made it safely to heaven. The next stories illustrate how Luca communicated that he was fine and safe, and there was nothing to worry about. He would always be near his parents. A month after Luca passed away, Rosa and Vince went on a cruise, to try and get away from all the pain they were experiencing. They were allocated cabin 1177 and one night, they had a phone call at 10.55pm: Luca passed away at 10.55am. When Rosa answered the phone, she realised there was a little boy on the other end of the phone saying hello. Rosa replied, and the little boy continued to only say hello. This went on for a while and he just ended the call. When Rosa finished the call, "Who was on the telephone?" Vince asked.

"You are never going to believe me, but a little boy only saying hello." Rosa instinctively knew when they were allocated their cabin 1177, unexplained occurrences would happen, and they did. Luca was born on a full moon, and when Rosa was having trouble sleeping, she would stare at the moon from her bedroom window. On the cruise, there was a full moon and she would stare and take photos of the moon from the deck of the ship and when she developed the photos, she could see orbs in them.

On the third anniversary of Luca's passing, Rosa released balloons at the cemetery, and they got stuck in a tree. I said to Rosa:

"He was laughing at what happened with the balloon".

After church, Rosa was keen to come and see me for a one-on-one session, but there were no vacancies for that year. At Christmas 2015, Rosa told her family that she was not celebrating Christmas that year, and she was spending the day at the cemetery. On Christmas day, my mother-in-law and my husband decided to go the cemetery, which incidentally is a short walk from where I live, to visit their family who had passed away that year too. I am always busy on Christmas Day, because it is celebrated at our place, but I had an overwhelming feeling to go with my family to the cemetery. We were walking to the graves of my husband's family when I was compelled to go and look at some graves off to the left. When, I approached them, I noticed they were graves of children who had passed. I saw a woman sitting in front of a grave, but I didn't take any notice. Whilst I was walking away this lady looked up and asked if my name was Judy.

"Yes, I am Judy, but I am sorry I don't know who you are?"

"My name is Rosa, you read for me at church, many months ago and brought through my son Luca." I understood this was the lady I met at church. I walked over to her and gave her a hug. She told me an amazing story. Rosa said she had been sitting in front of Luca's grave all day and said:

"Okay Luca give me a sign that you're okay, " and at that moment, I walked past her. She was in shock and thought *what are the chances of this happening?* I remember asking my mother-in-law about the section I had come across and she said it was the baby section, and I instantly knew then, why I was compelled to go to the cemetery this year. Rosa was desperate to receive a sign from her beloved baby boy, and Luca didn't disappoint.

I have had many private readings with Rosa over the years and it never ceases to amaze me how our loved ones warn us of things to come. Rosa had a reading in early 2018 and at the time Luca spoke of a condition near her neck. I told Rosa, Luca said she had to get her neck checked. At the time Rosa was confused, because she did not have any symptoms around the neck area. A few months later, Rosa contacted me saying Luca was right. She hadn't been feeling well and went to the doctors who sent her to a specialist to check her neck out.

After some tests, the specialist discovered she had growths on the left side of her throat, and they needed to be operated on. I was blown away.

"It is all thanks to Luca, without him you may not have known to go seek medical advice regarding your neck." We both were astonished and knew that this beautiful baby boy helped his mum in a way that could never be repaid. Rosa mentioned when the doctors discovered she was sick and needed treatment, Vince and Rosa were hearing Luca's original song *My Name Is Luka* all the time. Vince's brother Joe had died when he was twenty-three and the days leading up to her second operation, she saw a car with the number plate *JOEY 21*. Furthermore, Vince had seen this car drive pass their home. Vince recognised this was a sign, Luca and his brother Joe would be watching over Rosa to help her to get through her operation.

Rosa asked me to do a charity night in honour of Luca and I agreed. The night proved to be exactly what Rosa and I hoped for, and spirit did not disappoint. There were many children in spirit present that night, and they were eager to speak with their loved ones on earth. Rosa spoke to me later and mentioned her friend who was a little sceptical had come to the night, but after her two sons came through with information only she would know, she left with a smile from ear to ear with the knowledge her two boys were with her, and their love never dies. Some of the proceedings and raffle Rosa organised went towards support packages for premature babies in Luca's name and given to a hospital in support of the charity.

Coincidently, World Premature Baby Day is on the seventeenth of November, and this is the anniversary of Rosa's dad's death. Luca was also born on Vince's brother's birthday.

My children often ask me why I do the work I do. My answer is simple: I love spirit and I love bringing through their love to the families left behind on earth. It is pleasure and an honour to validate our loved ones in heaven. They never die, so love never dies and it is incredible how spirit orchestrates and synchronises events to help bring people together. I cannot thank Luca enough for his messages and feeling the love he has for his mother. I have no words. He is a special little boy with an enormous compacity to give and the unconditional love he shares with Rosa is miraculous. He continues to help Rosa with her health and is always there to let her know not to give up and keep living because, in my experience, that is what spirit always wants us to do. I have a son, and I know a mother's love for a child is unconditional and to lose a child at a such a young age is incomprehensible. What Rosa and Luca have shown me is that even though we are going through tough times in our lives, there are days to live for, and our loved ones will always be by our side and give us signs that they are here beside us and they are happy and loved.

Great Uncle Laurie

My last story is a fun story and it is about a family friend and his Great-Uncle Laurie. Shaun is quite the larrikin, and a typical dinky-di Aussie. I have known Shaun and his family for many years. My daughter's dance at the same dance studio owned by his wife, Megan. When I first meet people, I am reluctant to mention what I do for a profession, because some people are not as open minded as others. But when I do meet likeminded people, we click straight away and we can talk about everything to do with spirit, and nine times out of ten, they have had similar experiences with spirit, as I have, and they have exciting stories to share.

I first met Shaun when I saw him dropping off his kids at the same time as my children at dance class, and I remember he was always a fun-loving guy and loved to talk to everyone and this hasn't changed. One night, he said he had experienced spirits in his house, and I was intrigued because this was down my avenue. We struck up a conversation, and I told him I was a professional medium and as they say the rest was history.

Shaun has had a couple of private readings with me over the years and during one session, his Great Uncle Laurie made an appearance. Shaun spoke about his family being buried at the local cemetery - the cemetery located a short walk from my home. He knew his Great Uncle Laurie was buried there, however; he did not know the exact location.

Around two in the afternoon one day in late 2016, Shaun decided to go to the cemetery and visit his Grandfather Harry along with his Uncle Tommy. The day was quite hot, and Shaun had been at the graveyard for about twenty minutes. He decided to try and locate his Great Uncle Laurie's gravesite to say g'day and let him know that he had always thought about him along with his other family members. He had never tracked down his uncle's grave, but he was eager to find it.

Shaun called his mum and asked her where his great uncle's grave was placed. She told him to drive straight up the hill from where he was standing and at the end of the road, turn right. She said once you turned right, pull over, go left and he is near a big tree.

Shaun followed his mother's instructions. He jumped out of the car and started to walk towards some big trees he couldn't track down the grave straight away and he said, he walked around like a lost sheep trying to find this grave site.

Finally, Shaun, went back to his car to ring his mother a second time and she gave him the same directions. He became frustrated when he couldn't find this grave site, and at the same time he noticed a black crow not far from him and it was squawking. Shaun remembers saying how loud it was, and how he wished it would get lost.

It was a very hot day, but Shaun did not want to give up the search for his great uncle's burial place. He started yelling to his Great Uncle Laurie: okay Uncle Laurie, give me a sign. The crow was still squawking. I have always spoken to my clients about black crows and magpies: they are signs from our loved ones in heaven, and a magpie is my Nanna Blair's way of giving me a sign. These birds, in my belief are our loved ones: my nan comes in the form a of a bird to let me know she is around.

Shaun walked back to his car, and when he looked around the black crow was still squawking. He recalled what I had said about these birds and he started to walk towards the black crow, and the bird immediately moved towards a large tree. When it stopped at a particular tree near the location Shaun been searching, it stopped squawking. He strolled to where the black crow was sitting and walked past it. When he looked at the bottom of this tree, he couldn't find anything, and he became exasperated. The black crow started squawking again and Shaun walked four to five metres away from the bird. As Shaun approached the bird, it flew over his shoulder. When he looked down, he caught sight of a grave and recognised the name: it was his Great Uncle Laurie's grave. Shaun realised, the black crow was a sign from his family and when he looked around to thank the bird, he noticed the black crow was flying in the direction of my home. He quickly telephoned me and told me about his experience. We were both amazed and thankful for Great Uncle Laurie - for showing Shaun where to find him. I want to thank Shaun and his great uncle for allowing me to share their story. It proves without a doubt, when we ask for signs from spirit, they will always deliver. It may not be in the way we expect, but if we have an open mind - ask and you shall receive.

30

Labour of Love

I have never understood the phrase labour of love until now. As you all know, my gift is my passion and my professional work is my love. My best friend, Emma, accurately portrayed me when she wrote in the foreword of this book. She spoke about how my second book is highly personal and I totally agree, because what I have learnt whilst writing my first book and my second book is phenomenal. My own spiritual growth throughout my career has shaped the person I am today and the love and respect I have for the spirit world and God in indescribable.

The world through my eyes is incredible, and I have come to understand, the world is not one dimensional: it is multi-dimensional, and sometimes we see what we want to see, or experience only what we want to experience. But the physical life is only one part of our souls' journey here on Earth. There is life after life. When we learn to accept the person and environment we live in, we see and experience life with a better understanding. A new life that is filled with wonder emerges, and as we gaze on the experiences we have learnt, plus memories we have encountered, our soul begins to shine, and we can take steps towards developing our soul and a life worth living.

Whilst writing this book, I have undergone a massive transformation. Even though I didn't know it at the time, these transformations have made room for larger opportunities that I didn't know existed unless I accepted my journey and let go of the past and embraced the future. I also had to learn to relinquish control. The biggest lesson I have learnt throughout my transformation, is to accept myself and to know, I am not in control of everything in my life. What I have control over is knowing how to honour and respect myself, because at the end of the day - I am who I am meant to be in Gods eyes.

I could think of no better way to finish this book than with a phrase that encompasses who I am. It was given to me by my Angels.

I am what I am
I am all that I am
I do what I can
And
I honour and respect myself.

To everyone who has given their time to read my story, I thank you from the bottom of my heart.

Judy x

www.ingramcontent.com/pod-product-compliance
Lightning Source LLC
Chambersburg PA
CBHW050313010526
44107CB00055B/2223